The Easiest
AIR FRYER
KETO
Book ever!

THE EASIEST AIR FRYER KETO BOOK EVER!

4 Ingredients
PO Box 400
Caloundra QLD 4551
+61 431 297 923
ABN: 17 435 679 521

- 4ingredients.com.au
- facebook.com/4ingredientspage
- 4 ingredients Channel
- @4ingredients
- @4ingredients
- 4 Ingredients
- info@4ingredients.com.au

Copyright © Meymott Enterprises Pty Ltd

Published by 4 Ingredients August 2021

The moral right of the Author has been asserted.

All rights reserved. Without limiting the rights under copyright reserved above, no part of this publication may be reproduced, stored in or introduced into a retrieval system, or transmitted, in any form or by any means (electronic, mechanical, multi-media, photocopying, recording, or otherwise), without the prior written permission of the Author and the publisher (Author) of this book.

Photography:	Justin Horsfall – outpoint.com.au
Design:	Shem Hunter – shemhunter.com
Publisher:	4 Ingredients – 4ingredients.com.au
Distribution:	Simon & Schuster, Australia
	Simon & Schuster, New Zealand
ISBN:	978-0-6489477-1-4

Every effort has been made to ensure the information contained in this book is complete and accurate.

The information in this publication is representative of the author's opinions and views. It is meant for educational and informational purposes only, and is not meant to prevent, diagnose, treat or cure any disease. The content should not be construed as professional medical advice.

The Author is not responsible for any specific health or allergy needs that may require medical supervision and is not responsible for any adverse reactions to the recipes within.

Should the reader need professional assistance, a qualified physician or health care practitioner should be consulted.

The Easiest AIR FRYER KETO Book ever!

Lamb Kebabs	62
Mushroom Parmigiana	64
Air Fryer Stuffed Mushrooms	65
Mustard Wings	66
Pork Mince Patties	68
Spring Vegetable Quiche	70
Steak Burgers	72
Eggplant Fries	74
Swede Fries	74
Parmesan Zucchini Fries	75

SIDES — 76

90-Second Keto Bread	78
Bacon Balsamic Brussels Sprouts	80
Garlic Green Beans	82
Asparagus with Parmesan & Pork Crackle	84
Seasoned Broccolini	86

DINNER — 90

Baked Ricotta with Lemon & Capers	92
Cauliflower Pizza Crusts	94
Cheesy Capsicum Eggs	96
Chicken Mignon	98
Chicken Pesto Pizza	100
Garlic & Herb Boerewors	102
Italian Steak Rolls	104
Jalapeño Hassleback Chicken	106
Moroccan Salmon	108
Naked Cheeseburgers	110
Pesto Parmesan Lamb Cutlets	112
Pizza Meatballs	114
Roast Chicken	116
Salmon Patties	118
Southern Fried Drumsticks	120
Stuffed Sausages	122
Zucchini Boats	124

DESSERT — 126

Air Fryer Cheesecake Bites	128
Berry Cobbler	130
Chocolate Bundt Cake	132
Giant Choc Chip Cookie	134
Giant PB Cookie	136
Vanilla Strawberry Cream Cake	138

Please Join Us	140
BIBLIOGRAPHY	**141**
INDEX	**142**

Index

Introduction 3
Guide to Weights & Measures 4
Contents 5
The Rise & Continued Rise of the Air Fryer 6
Cooking Times & Temperatures 8
Healthy Keto Air Frying 10

Blackened Salmon 11
Cream Cheese & Salmon Bagels 11
Haloumi & Toms 11

BREAKFAST 12
Air Fryer Boiled Egg & Crispy Bacon 14
Bacon & Egg Bites 16
Baked Avocado Eggs 18
Easy Homemade Granola 20
Ham & Egg Cup 22
Keto Bagels 24
Smashed Avo on Cauliflower Hash Browns 26

SNACKS 28
Avocado Wafers 30
Baked Feta 32
Chorizo Chips 34
Crispy Salami Roll-Ups 36
Salsa Topped Haloumi Wedges 38
Jalapeño Cheesy Bread 40
Parmesan Crusted Olives 42
Prosciutto Wrapped Brie 44
Steak & Mushroom Bites 46
Sweet Jalapeño Poppers 48

LUNCH 50
Antipasto Kebabs 52
Baked Avocado with Salmon 54
Coconut Prawns 56
Eggplant Pizza 58
Keto Chicken Tenders 60

Bibliography

Websites

Fork To Spoon – Your Guide to Everything Air Frying
www.forktospoon.com

How do Air Fryers Work?
www.fryerhouse.com/how-does-a-hot-air-fryer-work

Air Fryer Tips & Recipes
www.facebook.com/groups/1522233111383384

Must Try Healthy Air Fryer Recipes
www.fitmencook.com/healthy-air-fryer-recipes

35 Air Fryer Recipes That Will Make Eating Healthy Way More Delicious
www.delish.com/cooking/g4711/air-fryer-recipes

Kmart Air Fryer Recipes Australia
www.facebook.com/groups/157403764942418

Printable Cheat Sheet for Air Fryers
www.thirtyhandmadedays.com/cheat-sheet-for-air-fryers

Easy Air Fryer Keto Recipes
https://www.ketoconnect.net/air-fryer-biscuits/

Books & Magazines

McCosker, Kim. **The Easiest Air Fryer Book Ever!** 4 Ingredients. PO BOX 400. Caloundra Queensland 4551. Australia.

McCosker, Kim. **4 Ingredients.** 4 Ingredients. PO BOX 400. Caloundra Queensland 4551. Australia.

McCosker, Kim. **4 Ingredients MORE Gluten Free Lactose Free.** 4 Ingredients. PO BOX 400. Caloundra Queensland 4551. Australia.

McCosker, Kim. **4 Ingredients The Easiest ONE POT Cookbook Ever.** 4 Ingredients. PO BOX 400. Caloundra Queensland 4551. Australia.

CookSMARTS. **Air Fryer – Cooking Charts, Recipes & Hints.** CookSMARTS, 2020.

Dillard, Sam. **I love my Air Fryer Keto Diet Recipe Book.** Adams Media. 57 Littlefield Street Avon, Massachusetts 02322. Copyright at Simon & Schuster, Inc. 2019.

Dillard, Sam. **I love my Air Fryer Keto Diet 5 Ingredient Recipe Book.** Adams Media. 57 Littlefield Street Avon, Massachusetts 02322. Copyright at Simon & Schuster, Inc. 2019.

Please Join Us

4 Ingredients is a family of busy people bound together by the desire to create good, healthy, homemade meals quickly, easily and economically.

Our aim is to save us all precious time and money in the kitchen. If this is you too, then we invite you to join our growing family where we share kitchen wisdom daily.

Similarly, if you have a favourite recipe or a tip that has worked for you in the kitchen and think others would enjoy it too, we'd love to hear from you:

 facebook.com/4ingredientspage

 4 Ingredients Channel

 @4ingredients

 @4ingredients

 @4ingredients

 4ingredients.com.au

Vanilla Strawberry Cream Cake
Serves 6

The classic combination of strawberries and cream just gives everything a lift.

- 1 cup (100g) almond meal
- ½ cup (75g) Natvia
- 1 tsp. (5g) baking powder
- 2 tbsp. (40g) coconut oil (extra for greasing)
- 2 large eggs (51g each)
- 1 tsp. (5g) vanilla extract
- 300ml cold cream
- 200g fresh ripe strawberries

Preheat air fryer at 180ºC, for 3 minutes.

In a large bowl, mix together almond meal, Natvia and baking powder with a pinch of sea salt.

Add coconut oil, eggs and vanilla and stir to combine.

Lightly brush a 16cm cake tin with extra coconut oil.

Using a spatula, scrape the mixture into the cake tin.

Pop in the air fryer basket and cover with alfoil.

Cook at 160ºC, for 20 minutes.

Remove alfoil and cook for another 10 minutes or until a skewer inserted removes clean.

When cool, whip the cold cream with an electric beater for 5 minutes or until stiff peaks form.

Spread across the cake and arrange the sliced strawberries on top. Starting from the outside, use the larger slices (pointy side out) gradually working your way in. Overlap each layer to create height.

Nutritional Information

	Per Serve
Calories	362.5
Kilojoules	1522.6
Total Fat	35.8g
– Saturated Fat	18.7g
Sodium	141mg
Carbohydrates	3.8g
– Sugar	3.1g
Fibre	2.3g
Protein	6.9g

Giant PB Cookie
Serves 4

I know one giant cookie follows another, but they were both equally as good as each other, so I decided to include them both. Some prefer chocolate, some peanut butter...
Make them both and you decide.

- ⅓ cup (33g) almond meal
- 2 tbsp. (24g) Natvia
- 1 large egg (51g)
- 3 tbsp. (75g) crunchy peanut butter
- 1 tsp. (3g) cinnamon

Preheat air fryer at 180°C, for 3 minutes.

Place all ingredients in a bowl with a pinch of sea salt and mix to combine.

Spoon the mixture onto a round of baking paper and lightly push to spread, keeping the thickness of the mixture as even as possible.

Cook at 180°C, for 8 minutes.

Nutritional Information

	Per Serve
Calories	181.7
Kilojoules	763.3
Total Fat	15.1g
– Saturated Fat	2.2g
Sodium	108mg
Carbohydrates	3.3g
– Sugar	2g
Fibre	2.2g
Protein	7.5g

Giant Chocolate Chip Cookie
Serves 4

This is a delicious cookie. The almond meal makes it nice and moist, and it's a lovely way to end a yummy dinner. I served it whole and everyone tore a piece from it and with only 82 calories and 6g carbs / serve it was a crowd pleaser.

- ½ cups (50g) almond meal
- 2 tbsp. (24g) Natvia
- 1 large egg (51g)
- 2 tbsp. (40g) butter
- 2 tbsp. (30g) sugar-free, chocolate chips

Preheat air fryer at 180ºC, for 3 minutes.

Place all ingredients in a bowl with a pinch of salt and mix to combine.

Spoon the mixture onto a round of baking paper and lightly push to spread out, keeping the thickness of the mixture as even as possible.

Cover with foil, cook at 180ºC, for 6 minutes.

Remove foil, cook for another 2 minutes.

Serve warm.

Chocolate Chip Muffins
Makes 6

Preheat air fryer at 180ºC, for 3 minutes. Lightly mist 6 small silicone muffin cups.

In a bowl, combine 1 cup (100g) almond meal + 2 tbsp. (24g) Natvia + ½ tbsp. (9g) baking powder + ¼ tsp. (6g) sea salt + ½ cup (75g) sugar-free, chocolate chips.

Then stir in ¼ cup (65ml) unsweetened almond milk + 1 large egg (51g). Spoon evenly across muffin cups.

Place in air fryer and cook at 160ºC, for 10 minutes. Cool for 5 minutes, during which time they will continue to cook. Remove from cases when cool.

Nutritional Information

	Per Serve
Calories	198.3
Kilojoules	832.7
Total Fat	18.2g
– Saturated Fat	7.1g
Sodium	64.7mg
Carbohydrates	5.2g
– Sugar	4g
Fibre	1.3g
Protein	4.8g

Chocolate Bundt Cake
Serves 6

- 1½ cups (150g) almond meal
- ½ cup (75g) Natvia
- ⅓ cup (30g) unsweetened cocoa powder
- 1 tsp. (5g) baking powder
- ⅓ cup (85g) unsweetened almond milk
- 2 large eggs (51g each)
- 1 tsp. (5g) vanilla extract

Preheat air fryer at 180ºC, for 3 minutes.

In a large mixing bowl, stir all ingredients until well combined.

Spray a mini Bundt tin with oil.
NB: Bundt cake tins come in a variety of sizes, the size that you need will depend on the size of your air fryer. A light spray with oil, or brush with melted butter will prevent sticking.

Scoop the batter into the tin.

Place in the air fryer basket and cook at 160ºC, for 10 minutes. Cool for 5 minutes before removing.

SERVING SUGGESTION: For the photoshoot I simply spread the top with Vanilla COYO (coconut yoghurt) and scattered with edible flowers.

Nutritional Information

	Per Serve
Calories	200.7
Kilojoules	842.7
Total Fat	16.7g
– Saturated Fat	1.8g
Sodium	144mg
Carbohydrates	2.7g
– Sugar	1.5g
Fibre	3.6g
Protein	8.5g

Berry Cobbler
Serves 4

This is scrumptious!

- 2 cups (250g) frozen blueberries, thawed
- ½ cup (120g) softened butter
- ¼ cup (38g) Natvia
- 2 eggs (51g each)
- ½ cup (50g) almond meal
- 1 tsp. (5g) vanilla extract

Preheat air fryer at 180ºC, for 3 minutes.

Place the thawed blueberries into the base of an 8 x 8cm ceramic dish or loaf tin.

In a bowl, mix together remaining ingredients with a pinch of sea salt and spoon over blueberries.

Poke gently to mix slightly the berries and almond mixture.

Place the dish in the air fryer.

Cover with alfoil.

Bake at 180ºC, for 10 minutes. Remove foil and bake for another 5 minutes or until well browned.

Cool before removing.

SERVING SUGGESTION: Top with whipped cream or COYO and a sprinkle of cinnamon – YUMMY!

Nutritional Information

	Per Serve
Calories	358.1
Kilojoules	1503.9
Total Fat	33.6g
– Saturated Fat	17g
Sodium	180.7mg
Carbohydrates	7.1g
– Sugar	6.7g
Fibre	3.4g
Protein	6.5g

Air Fryer Cheesecake Bites
Makes 12

Literally every recipe in this chapter contains almond meal. Almond meal is a great gluten-free alternative to flour, and it's super-versatile to bake with. From moist cakes and giant cookies to bliss balls and cheesecake bites, almond meal forms the basis of them all.

- 200g cream cheese
- ½ cup (75g) Natvia
- 1 tsp. (5g) vanilla extract
- ½ cup (50g) almond meal

Preheat air fryer at 180°C, for 3 minutes.

Cut the cream cheese into cubes and place in a bowl.

Add the Natvia (reserving 2 tbsp. for later) and vanilla and mix together until nice and smooth. Refrigerate for 15 minutes.

Roll into 16 equal size balls.

In a small bowl, mix together the almond meal with 2 tbsp. Natvia.

Roll the cheesecake balls into the almond mixture, and lightly mist with coconut oil for a golden finish (optional).

Place 8 in the air fryer basket.

Cook at 160°C, for 5 minutes.

Repeat. Store in an air-tight container in the fridge.

23.1g Fat
9.7g Carbs

Chocolate Chip Cheesecake
Serves 4

In a bowl mix together 250g softened cream cheese and ½ cup (75g) Natvia until nice and creamy. Add 1 large egg (51g), 1 tsp. (5g) vanilla extract and ¼ cup (60g) sugar-free, chocolate chips and fold to combine.

Spoon the mixture into a 16cm baking dish. Cover with alfoil and cook at 160°C, for 10 minutes. Remove alfoil, reduce heat to 140°C and cook for 15 minutes.

Cool for 10 minutes, then refrigerate for at least 3 hours. Slice to serve.

Nutritional Information

	Per Serve
Calories	74.3
Kilojoules	311.9
Total Fat	7g
– Saturated Fat	3.1g
Sodium	53.6mg
Carbohydrates	0.4g
– Sugar	0.3g
Fibre	0.4g
Protein	2.3g

Dessert

Zucchini Boats
Serves 2

Thanks to my lovely girlfriend Jendy, whose hairdresser shared with her this deliciously easy recipe. I loved it as soon as I heard it, more when I ate it.

- 2 medium zucchinis (200g each)
- 2 tbsp. (40g) olive tapenade
- ¾ cup (90g) grated Parmesan

Slice each zucchini in half, lengthways.

Spread each flat side with tapenade, then sprinkle with Parmesan.

Season with cracked pepper.

Place in air fryer basket.

Bake at 180ºC, for 8 minutes.

Serve immediately with your favourite salad.

2-Ingredient Zucchini Crisps
Serves 2

9.3g Fat
1.7g Carbs

- 1 medium zucchini (200g)
- ½ cup (62g) grated Parmesan

Slice the zucchini into 1cm rounds. Sprinkle each round with Parmesan and season. Place into air fryer basket in single layer. Cook at 180ºC, for 8 to 10 minutes or until tender and golden.

Nutritional Information

	Per Serve
Calories	258
Kilojoules	1083.5
Total Fat	17.8g
– Saturated Fat	9.1g
Sodium	911.3mg
Carbohydrates	4.4g
– Sugar	3.7g
Fibre	2.4g
Protein	18.4g

Stuffed Sausages
Serves 2

- ½ onion, sliced (80g)
- ½ red capsicum, cut into strips (165g)
- 2 tbsp. (38g) butter, melted
- 1 tbsp. (23g) Dijon mustard
- 4 thick pork sausages (320g)

Preheat air fryer at 180ºC, for 3 minutes.

Line air fryer with baking paper.

In a bowl, mix onions, capsicum, butter and mustard together.

Season well.

Slice each sausage lengthways, 75% through.

Stuff each sausage with the onion mixture.

Place on baking paper in the air fryer basket.

Cook at 180ºC, for 10 minutes.

Nutritional Information

	Per Serve
Calories	479
Kilojoules	2011.9
Total Fat	37.4g
– Saturated Fat	14.1g
Sodium	1239.4mg
Carbohydrates	9.2g
– Sugar	7.6g
Fibre	4.6g
Protein	26.3g

Southern Fried Drumsticks
Serves 4

Not quite Colonel Sanders' 11 secret herbs and spices but much easier and delicious regardless.

- 1kg chicken drumsticks
- 2 tbsp. (36g) olive oil
- 1 tsp. (3g) garlic powder
- 1 tsp. (3g) paprika
- ½ tsp. (1g) cumin

Preheat air fryer at 180ºC, for 3 minutes.

In a small bowl, combine garlic, paprika and cumin with 1 tsp. each of sea salt and cracked pepper.

Place drumsticks in a bowl, drizzle with olive oil, and brush to coat completely.

Sprinkle with seasoning, tossing to coat completely.

Place drumsticks in air fryer basket, cook at 180ºC, for 20 minutes.

Turn and cook for another 20 minutes.

Nutritional Information

	Per Serve
Calories	446
Kilojoules	1873.4
Total Fat	31.2g
– Saturated Fat	8g
Sodium	157.6mg
Carbohydrates	0.9g
– Sugar	0.4g
Fibre	0.5g
Protein	41.4g

Salmon Patties

Serves 4

Yes, these use a can of salmon and they are AH-MAZING! Don't forget that canned salmon is rich in protein, vitamin D, calcium (from the bones) and heart healthy Omega-3 fats. Canned or fresh, there is goodness in salmon!

- 415g can pink salmon, drained
- ¼ cup (60g) mayonnaise
- 1 large egg (51g)
- 2 tsp. (8g) lemon zest
- ½ cup (50g) almond meal
- 2 tbsp. (23g) capers, drained and chopped

In a bowl, place all ingredients and season with cracked pepper.

Mix to combine well.

Roll into 8 patties.

Place 4 patties into the air fryer basket and cook at 180ºC, 5 minutes.

Gently flip and cook for another 5 minutes.

Transfer to a large serving dish and repeat with remaining 4 patties.

SERVING SUGGESTION: Serve with a little Tartare sauce and a fresh salad.

Nutritional Information

	Per Serve
Calories	335.3
Kilojoules	1408.2
Total Fat	24.3g
– Saturated Fat	3.9g
Sodium	369.3mg
Carbohydrates	2.2g
– Sugar	2.6g
Fibre	1.6g
Protein	27.2g

Roast Chicken
Serves 6

After experimenting, I discovered that if I left the legs up the chicken legs got way overcooked. Breast side down for the first 40 to 50 minutes of cooking time keeps everything nice and moist.

- 2kg whole chicken
- 2 tbsp. (36g) olive oil
- 1 tsp. (3g) garlic powder
- 1 tsp. (3g) smoked paprika
- 1 tsp. (3g) dried Italian herbs

Combine the seasonings with the oil.

Add 1 tbsp. sea salt and 1 tsp. cracked pepper to make a paste and spread it all over the chicken.

Spray the air fryer basket with oil.

Place the chicken in the basket breast side down and cook at 180ºC, for 50 minutes.

Carefully flip the chicken to breast side up and cook for an additional 10 minutes.

Sit for 10 minutes before carving to serve.

Nutritional Information

	Per Serve
Calories	222
Kilojoules	2932.5
Total Fat	35.9g
– Saturated Fat	9.2g
Sodium	1434.3mg
Carbohydrates	0.7g
– Sugar	0.3g
Fibre	4g
Protein	91.8g

Pizza Meatballs
Serves 4

Pizza and Meatballs in the same sentence, I know right? This is a PAR-TAY we all want an invite to!

- 500g lean beef mince
- 1 large egg (51g)
- ¼ cup (70g) sun-dried tomato pesto
- ½ cup (60g) grated mozzarella cheese

In a large bowl, place all ingredients and season with sea salt and cracked pepper.

Roll to form into 6cm size meatballs.

Place in the air fryer basket.

Cook at 200ºC, for 6 minutes.

Shake and cook for another 6 to 8 minutes, or until cooked through.

OPTIONAL: Warm a jar of passata or your favourite pasta sauce. Spread across a plate or into a bowl and pile the meatballs high.

Nutritional Information

	Per Serve
Calories	309.5
Kilojoules	1300
Total Fat	18.7g
– Saturated Fat	7.6g
Sodium	388.1mg
Carbohydrates	1.7g
– Sugar	1.1g
Fibre	0.4g
Protein	33.7g

Pesto Parmesan Lamb Cutlets
Serves 2

- 4 lamb cutlets (300g)
- 2 tbsp. (46g) basil pesto
- 2 tbsp. (40g) grated Parmesan

Preheat air fryer at 180°C, for 3 minutes.

Place lamb cutlets in the air fryer.

Cook at 200°C, for 5 minutes.

Mix together basil pesto and Parmesan cheese and season with cracked pepper.

Turn cutlets, top with pesto mixture.

Cook for 7 minutes.

Rest for 5 minutes before removing to serve.

Prosciutto & Pesto Cutlets
Serves 2

- 4 lamb cutlets (216g)
- 4 slices prosciutto (70g)
- 2 tbsp. (46g) basil pesto

Preheat air fryer at 180°C, for 3 minutes. Place lamb cutlets in the air fryer. Cook at 200°C, for 5 minutes. Meanwhile lay 4 strips of prosciutto onto a clean surface. Using tongs, remove cutlets, lay each onto a strip of prosciutto. Dollop each cutlet with Basil Pesto, wrap with prosciutto. Return to the air fryer basket and cook at 180°C, for 7 minutes. Rest for 5 minutes before removing to serve.

Nutritional Information

	Per Serve
Calories	416.4
Kilojoules	1748.7
Total Fat	28.4g
– Saturated Fat	10.g
Sodium	657.1mg
Carbohydrates	1.1g
– Sugar	0.8g
Fibre	0.4g
Protein	38.9g

Naked Cheeseburgers
Serves 4

These were good! I first tried a 'naked burger' at the world famous In-N-Out Burger in Los Angeles over 10 years ago – I could not believe how good a burger tasted without a bun! The burger recipe is from The Easiest Air Fryer Book Ever! But rather than a bun, it is housed in a lettuce cup.

- 500g lean beef mince
- 2 tbsp. (46g) Dijon mustard
- 2 tbsp. (50g) Worcestershire sauce
- 4 large lettuce leaves (60g)
- 4 cheddar cheese slices (84g)
- 4 whole pickles (25g each)

In a large bowl, mix the mince, Dijon and Worcestershire with 1 tsp. each of sea salt and cracked pepper together.

Form into 4 thick, round patties.

Place into the air fryer basket.

Cook at 180ºC, for 8 minutes, flip then cook for another 8 minutes.

Place a square of cheddar cheese on each and rest for 5 minutes.

Serve with a pickle (or 2) and a dollop of mustard, some lettuce and crispy bacon.

OPTIONAL: Don't forget to wash thoroughly the air fryer basket after cooking. There may be a lot of juice in its base, that if left for the next time you cook something, may smoke.

Mexican Burgers
Serves 4

Combine 500g lean beef mince with 1 medium carrot and 1 medium zucchini, both grated and a 35g packet MAGGI Chilli Con Carne seasoning in bowl.

Use hands to mix until well combined. Shape the mixture into 4 patties.

Cook at 180ºC, for 8 minutes, flip then cook for another 8 minutes.

Nutritional Information

	Per Serve
Calories	285.3
Kilojoules	1198.4
Total Fat	11.8g
– Saturated Fat	6.2g
Sodium	766.1mg
Carbohydrates	10.1g
– Sugar	8.8g
Fibre	0.9g
Protein	34.5g

Moroccan Salmon
Serves 2

For the fastest meal ever, salmon in the air fryer fits the bill. Literally 10 minutes is all that is required for a perfectly tender, deliciously crusted piece of salmon.

- 2 large salmon fillets (440g)
- 1 tsp. (18g) olive oil spray
- 1 tbsp. Moroccan seasoning

Lightly mist the salmon and season generously with Moroccan seasoning and cracked pepper.

Arrange salmon in air fryer basket.

Cook at 180ºC, for 12 minutes or until it flakes easily (depending on its size).

Sweet Mustard Salmon
Serves 2

34.7g Fat
3.4g Carbs

Try this; this sweet mustard topping makes this one of our favourite salmon dishes.

- 2 large salmon fillets (440g)
- 1 tsp. (4.6g) olive oil
- 2 tbsp. (46g) wholegrain mustard
- 1 tbsp. (12g) Natvia
- 1 garlic clove, crushed (3g)
- ½ tsp. (1.3g) thyme leaves

In a small bowl, whisk together all ingredients. Spread on top of salmon and cook at 180ºC, for 12 minutes.

Nutritional Information

	Per Serve
Calories	560.1
Kilojoules	2352.6
Total Fat	40.2g
– Saturated Fat	8.9g
Sodium	1192.2mg
Carbohydrates	4.8g
– Sugar	2.3g
Fibre	1.2g
Protein	45.5g

Jalapeño Hasselback Chicken
Serves 2

There are so many Hasselback chicken variations done in the air fryer, something about the way it cooks, it is just so juicy and tender. This is just another that my family really enjoyed.

- 2 slices rindless bacon (50g each)
- 4 tbsp. (80g) cream cheese, softened
- ¼ cup (40g) pickled jalapeños, chopped
- ½ cup (60g) grated cheddar cheese
- 2 boneless, skinless chicken breasts (500g)

Preheat air fryer at 180ºC, for 3 minutes.

In a medium bowl, stir together bacon, cream cheese, jalapeños, and half the cheddar cheese.

Cut about 6 slits across the top of each breast, 2cm apart and 75% through.

Stuff the cream cheese mixture into the slits.

Sprinkle with remaining cheese.

Place in air fryer basket, cook at 180ºC, for 20 minutes or until the cheese has melted and juices run clear.

SERVING SUGGESTION: Serve with your favourite garden salad and Swede Fries (see p. 74).

Nutritional Information

	Per Serve
Calories	619.9
Kilojoules	2603.5
Total Fat	33.6g
– Saturated Fat	18.1g
Sodium	1267.4mg
Carbohydrates	3.2g
– Sugar	3g
Fibre	0.3g
Protein	76g

Italian Steak Rolls
Serves 2

These Italian Steak Rolls are stuffed with green spinach, marinated capsicums and mozzarella cheese and are easily made in your air fryer! It's one of those dishes that seems fancy but actually isn't and is one everyone seems to love.

- 2 long minute steaks (200g each)
- 1 tbsp. (18g) olive oil
- 1 garlic clove, crushed (3g)
- 1 tbsp. (10g) Italian seasoning
- 1 cup (45g) English spinach
- 4 strips marinated capsicum (80g)
- 2 tbsp. (40g) grated mozzarella cheese

Place the steaks onto a plate and bring to room temperature.

Mix together the olive oil, crushed garlic and seasoning.

Brush to coat the steaks. Season with sea salt and cracked pepper.

Ensure the steak is covered and marinate for 30 minutes.

Preheat air fryer at 180ºC, for 3 minutes.

Then, place the steak on a flat surface.

Spread with spinach, then capsicums and cheese.

Roll up as tightly as you can.

Place in air fryer basket, seam side down.

Cook at 200ºC, for 7 to 8 minutes, or until done.

Rest for 5 minutes before slicing to serve.

Nutritional Information

	Per Serve
Calories	418.8
Kilojoules	1759
Total Fat	18.8g
– Saturated Fat	6.3g
Sodium	305.6mg
Carbohydrates	7.3g
– Sugar	3.2g
Fibre	2.2g
Protein	54.4g

Garlic & Herb Boerewors
Serves 4

I first saw a Boerewors sausage at Justine Davies' house in Johannesburg, Christmas 1990. I couldn't believe how long it was. Boerewors are a South African (and Namibian) BBQ classic, they are shaped into a continuous spiral around a foot in diameter, and they are lovely. I bought this one at my local Aldi thinking it would work in my air fryer – it did!

- 500g Boerewors
- 1 tbsp. (18g) olive oil spray
- 1 tsp. rosemary leaves, chopped
- 1 tsp. (3g) thyme leaves

Lightly mist the sausage, season with sea salt and pepper and rosemary.

Place in air fryer basket.

Cook at 180°C, for 7 minutes. Flip, season with thyme and cook for a further 7 minutes or until well-browned on the outside and cooked through.

OPTIONAL: Sprinkle with some finely chopped garlic before cooking.

9.8g Fat
30.5g Carbs

Crispy Gnocchi

We know this is not Keto, Gnocchi generally needing some element of flour to bind. However, after much discussion we decided to include it regardless as we all really like 'Crispy Gnocchi'.

Toss 200g gnocchi in 1 tbsp. (18g) olive oil, season with ½ tsp. (1.3g) garlic powder and ½ tsp. (3g) sea salt. Transfer to the basket of your air fryer. Cook at 180°C, for 12 minutes, shaking every 4 minutes. Serve with your favourite Pasta Sauce and steamed greens.

Nutritional Information

	Per Serve
Calories	30.5
Kilojoules	1218.3
Total Fat	24.7g
– Saturated Fat	9.5g
Sodium	775.6mg
Carbohydrates	1.4g
– Sugar	1.3g
Fibre	3g
Protein	18.2g

Chicken Pesto Pizza
Serves 2

Aren't they just 3 of the loveliest words? They don't disappoint when combined to create this yummy dinner either!

- 2 boneless, skinless chicken thigh fillets (350g)
- 2 tbsp. (50g) basil pesto
- ½ cup (60g) grated mozzarella cheese
- 4 cherry tomatoes, sliced (32g)

Preheat air fryer at 180ºC, for 3 minutes.

Lightly mallet the thighs to flatten slightly.

Brush each flattened side with basil pesto.

Sprinkle with grated cheese and dot with rounds of tomatoes.

Cook at 180ºC, for 10 minutes.

Rest for 3 minutes, check for doneness.

27.7g Fat
0.4g Carbs

Air Fryer Chicken Parcels
Serves 4

Cut 2 chicken breasts (500g) into large bite-size pieces. Spread with 2 tbsp. (40g) softened cream cheese. Season with sea salt and cracked pepper. Wrap each in bacon (128g) securing with a toothpick. Place pieces in the air fryer basket and cook at 180ºC, for 6 minutes. Flip each of the pieces and cook for a further 2 minutes or until done. Serve warm.

Nutritional Information

	Per Serve
Calories	396.8
Kilojoules	1666.8
Total Fat	25.6g
– Saturated Fat	8.4g
Sodium	569.7mg
Carbohydrates	1.9g
– Sugar	1.2g
Fibre	0.6g
Protein	39.7g

Chicken Mignon
Serves 2

Chicken Mignon is one of our family's favourite meals. It's that delicious combination of moist chicken thighs, wrapped in bacon, with a delicious garlic butter centre... Oh! I think I might just have to make it for dinner tonight!

- 3 tbsp. (60g) butter
- 2 garlic cloves, crushed (6g)
- 1 tsp. (3g) thyme leaves
- 2 slices rindless bacon (50g each)
- 2 boneless, skinless chicken thigh fillets (350g)

Preheat air fryer at 180ºC, for 3 minutes.

In a bowl, mix together the butter, crushed garlic and thyme and season.

Lay each slice of bacon onto a clean, dry surface.

Lightly mallet the thighs to flatten slightly. Brush each flattened side with the infused butter.

Roll up the chicken thigh and place it onto a long length of bacon, roll the bacon around the thigh and fasten it together with a toothpick.

Evenly dollop remaining infused butter across both.

Place in air fryer basket and cook at 180ºC, for 10 minutes.

Check for doneness, remove toothpicks before serving.

SERVING SUGGESTION: Serve with steamed greens, roasted tomatoes and mashed sweet potato.

Nutritional Information

	Per Serve
Calories	458.3
Kilojoules	1924.8
Total Fat	31.6g
– Saturated Fat	12.3g
Sodium	961.1mg
Carbohydrates	1g
– Sugar	0.4g
Fibre	1g
Protein	42.9g

Cheesy Capsicum Eggs
Serves 2

Green capsicums are picked to promote growth in the plant. They are more bitter in taste compared to the riper redder capsicums but offer a delicious flavour in omelettes, baked, or scattered across the top of your favourite pizza.

- 2 green capsicums (250g each)
- 2 large eggs, whisked (51g each)
- 40g cooked ham off the bone
- ½ cup (60g) grated cheddar cheese

Cut the top off the capsicum and remove the membrane.

Divide ham and cheese across each.

Divide egg mixture evenly into each capsicum.

Top each with a sprinkle of cheese.

Season.

Bake at 180ºC, for 10 minutes or until tender.

THE SECRET INGREDIENT IS ALWAYS *cheese*

Nutritional Information

	Per Serve
Calories	264.3
Kilojoules	1110
Total Fat	15.3g
– Saturated Fat	7.6g
Sodium	627.5mg
Carbohydrates	7.2g
– Sugar	7.1g
Fibre	5.9g
Protein	22.1g

Cauliflower Pizza Crusts
Serves 4

This grain free and healthy pizza base is relatively easy to make, the flip can be a little tricky, but using two pieces of baking paper makes it easier.

- 500g frozen cauliflower rice, thawed
- 1 tbsp. (18g) olive oil spray
- 1 cup (120g) grated cheddar cheese
- 2 tbsp. (16g) almond meal
- 2 large eggs, whisked (51g each)
- 1 tsp. (3g) Italian seasoning

Line the air fryer basket with baking paper.

Squeeze excess moisture from the cauliflower.

Pat dry before placing in a large bowl.

Add cheese, almond meal, eggs and Italian seasoning and stir well.

Spoon mixture onto baking paper in the air fryer.

Press the dough down into an even shape covering the base of the air fryer basket.

Cook at 180ºC, for 12 minutes.

Remove, place another sheet of baking paper across the top.

Hold tightly, flip and place back in the air fryer (discard old baking paper).

Cook for another 6 minutes.

OPTIONAL: Top with whatever you like. Pizza Sauce, grated Mozzarella cheese, mushrooms, capsicum, salami etc. Place back into air fryer basket and cook an additional 4 minutes or until golden.

Toppings

For best results avoid oily ingredients, otherwise the crust gets even soggier. Toppings are endless, but two of my favourites are:

Pesto Chicken Pizza:
Spread with basil pesto, shredded chicken, spinach and mozzarella.

Margherita Pizza:
Pizza paste, mozzarella and basil leaves

Nutritional Information

	Per Serve
Calories	237.8
Kilojoules	998.8
Total Fat	17.9g
– Saturated Fat	7.1g
Sodium	356.9mg
Carbohydrates	5.2g
– Sugar	4.1g
Fibre	4g
Protein	13.6g

Baked Ricotta with Lemon & Capers
Serves 4

- 2 large eggs, whisked (51g each)
- 425g fresh whole-milk ricotta
- 2 tbsp. (10g) lemon zest
- 2 tbsp. (10g) thyme leaves

In a bowl combine the beaten eggs, ricotta cheese, lemon zest and thyme.

Season generously with sea salt and cracked pepper.

Line a 20cm round (or one that will fit in your air fryer) quiche dish with baking paper, or lightly mist with oil. Pour the mixture into it.

Transfer to the air fryer basket.

Cook at 180ºC, for 10 minutes, or until the top is nicely browned in spots.

Cool and gently remove; dish will be hot.

OPTIONAL: Add 2 tsp. capers and some fresh rosemary. Serve with a sprinkle of sea salt, cracked pepper and a smattering of lemon zest with a fresh garden salad.

Nutritional Information

	Per Serve
Calories	185.1
Kilojoules	777.4
Total Fat	12g
– Saturated Fat	6.9g
Sodium	200.3mg
Carbohydrates	4.2g
– Sugar	2.8g
Fibre	2g
Protein	13.6g

Dinner

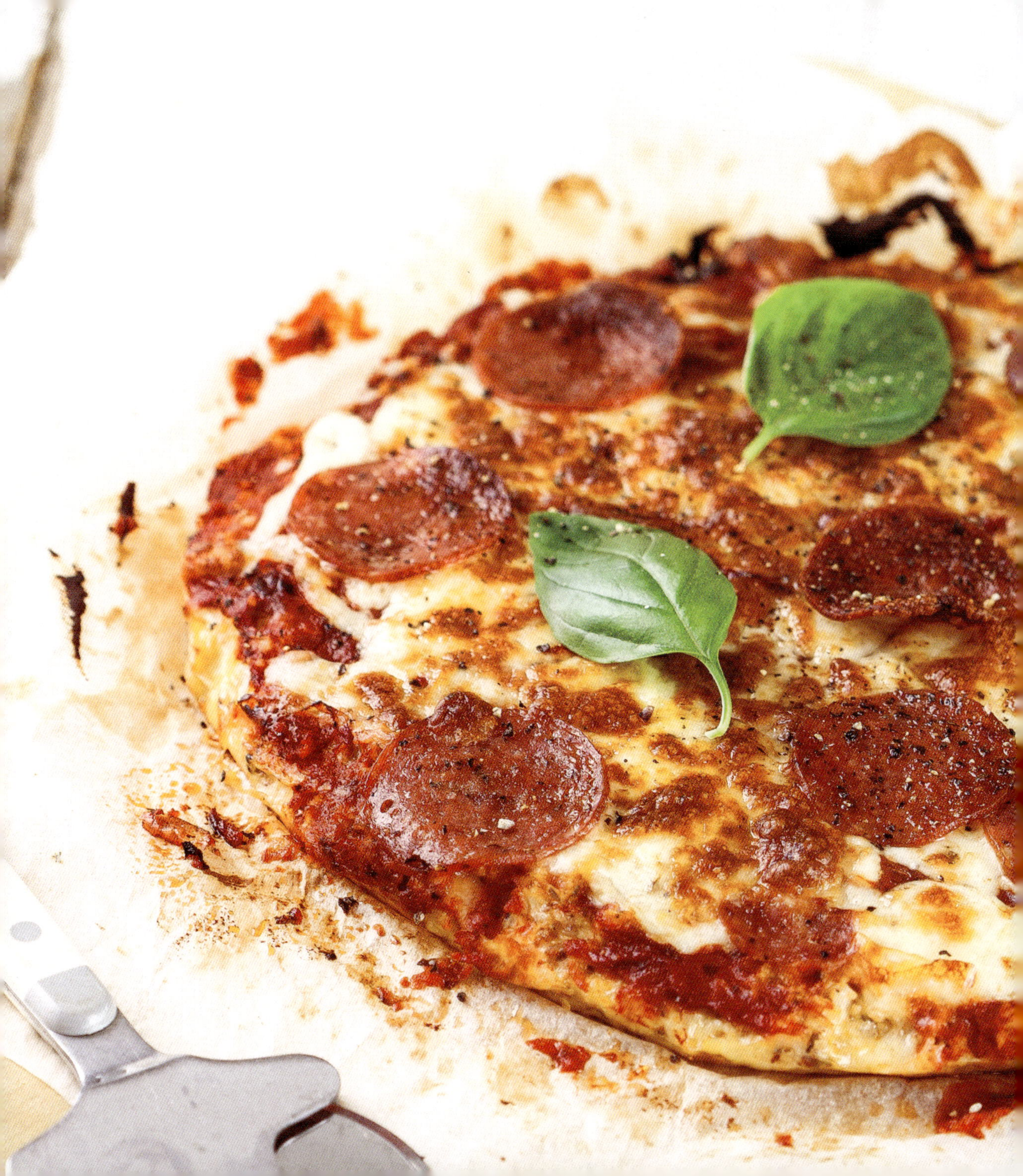

Bless the **FOOD** before us
the **FAMILY** beside us
& the **LOVE** between us

Amen

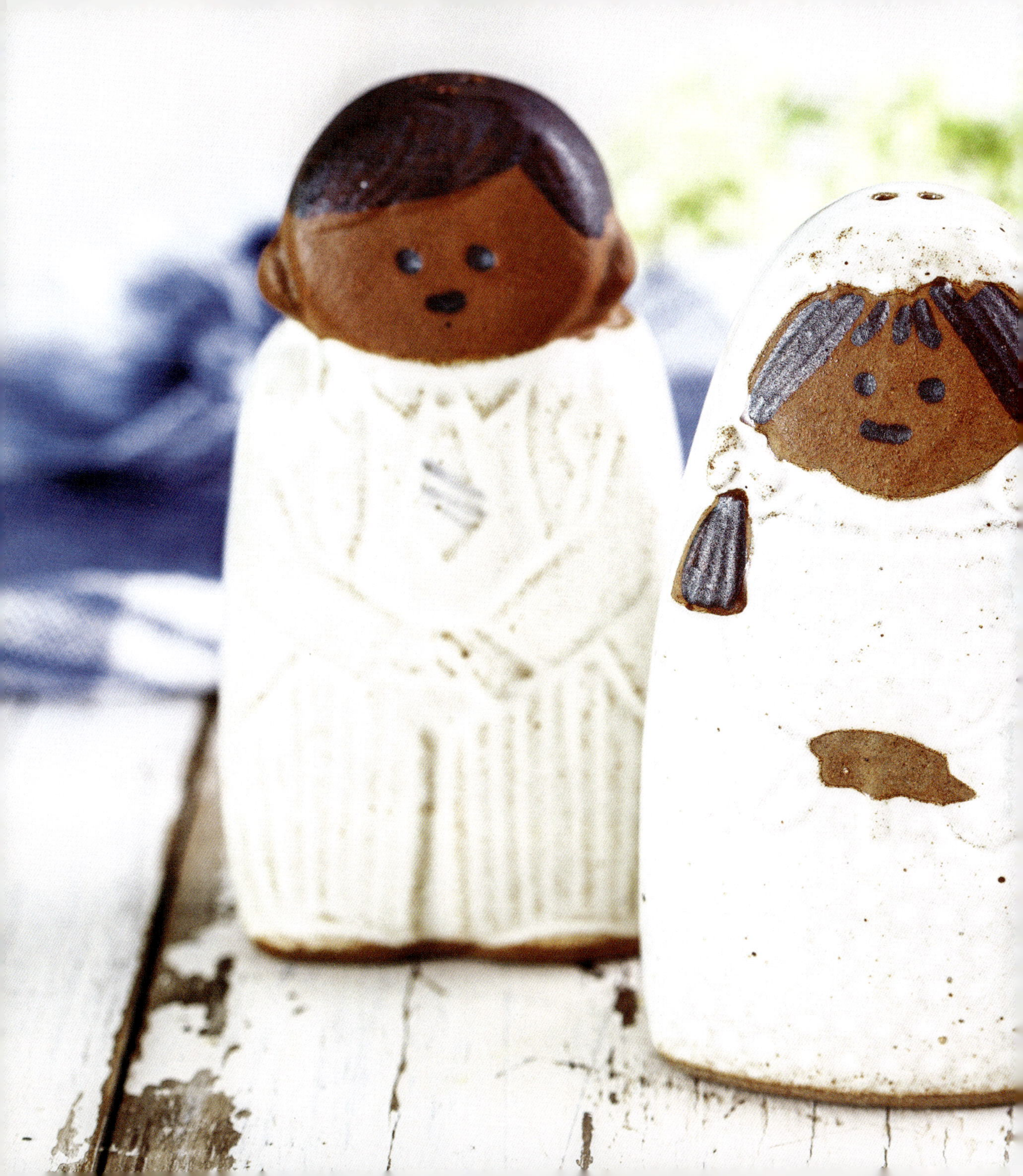

Seasoned Broccolini
Serves 4

- 2 bunches broccolini (348g)
- 1 tbsp. (18g) olive oil
- 2 garlic cloves, crushed (6g)
- 1 tbsp. (15g) nutritional yeast

Trim the woody ends off the broccolini.

In a medium-size bowl, toss the broccolini in olive oil, garlic and nutritional yeast.

Season with cracked pepper.

Place into the air fryer basket and cook at 160°C, for 4 minutes.

Flip and cook for another 3 minutes.

The broccolini should be crispy but cooked.

OPTIONAL: I have used Gourmet Garden's Stir-in Garlic Paste instead of garlic cloves.

Nutritional Information

	Per Serve
Calories	83.1
Kilojoules	348.9
Total Fat	5.2g
– Saturated Fat	0.8g
Sodium	15.3mg
Carbohydrates	3.2g
– Sugar	1.2g
Fibre	3.3g
Protein	5g

Asparagus with Parmesan & Pork Crackle

Serves 4

- 2 bunches fresh asparagus (130g each)
- 1 large egg, whisked (51g)
- ½ tsp. (1g) garlic powder
- ½ cup (12g) crushed pork rinds
- 2 tbsp. (40g) grated Parmesan

Line the air fryer with baking paper.

On a plate combine garlic powder, crushed pork rinds and Parmesan. Season with sea salt and cracked pepper.

Roll the asparagus spears in the egg wash, then in the seasoning.

Place in the air fryer basket. Cook at 180°C, for 4 minutes.

Turn and cook for an additional 4 minutes or until golden and crispy.

SERVING SUGGESTION: This is just lovely served with grilled chicken, pork or steak.

Nutritional Information

	Per Serve
Calories	85.5
Kilojoules	359
Total Fat	5g
– Saturated Fat	2.4g
Sodium	307.4mg
Carbohydrates	1.4g
– Sugar	1.1g
Fibre	1.6g
Protein	8.8g

Garlic Green Beans
Serves 4

- 250g fresh green beans, trimmed
- 1 tbsp. (18g) olive oil
- 1 tsp. (3g) garlic powder

Preheat air fryer at 180ºC, for 3 minutes.

Place the beans in a bowl.

Drizzle with oil and season with garlic powder.

Toss several times to coat.

Place in the air fryer basket.

Cook at 180ºC, for 6 minutes shaking halfway through for beans with a soft texture and crunch. Cook for 2 minutes more if you prefer softer beans.

4.7g Fat
2.2g Carbs

Blistered Green Beans
Serves 4

These blistered, crispy green beans are delicious, still juicy on the inside and perfectly done on the outside.

Make sure 200g beans are dry, dry beans fry crispier. Add to a bowl and drizzle with 1 tbsp. olive oil. Season with 1 tsp. sea salt, ½ tsp. pepper and a smattering of chilli flakes. Toss to combine, coating well. Place half the beans in an air fryer basket. Do not over crowd. Cook at 180ºC, for 8 minutes, shaking half way through. Repeat.

Nutritional Information

	Per Serve
Calories	58.6
Kilojoules	246
Total Fat	4.6g
– Saturated Fat	0.7g
Sodium	0.4mg
Carbohydrates	2.6g
– Sugar	1.9g
Fibre	1.9g
Protein	1.2g

Bacon Balsamic Brussels Sprouts
Serves 4

- 500g fresh medium brussels sprouts, trimmed and cut in half (about 4 cups)
- 1 tbsp. (18g) olive oil
- 2 slices rindless bacon, diced (100g)
- 1 tbsp. (20g) balsamic vinegar
- 2 tbsp. (40g) grated Parmesan

Add brussels sprouts to medium microwavable bowl; cover loosely with damp absorbent paper, and microwave on high for 7 minutes.

Drain and pat dry.

Drizzle with oil and season well with sea salt and cracked pepper.

Gently toss to coat.

Place sprouts in air fryer basket.

Cook at 180°C, for 6 minutes.

Shake basket; add bacon and cook for another 6 minutes or until sprouts are browned on edges, tender in the centre and bacon crispy.

Remove to a serving bowl, and toss with vinegar and Parmesan to serve.

TIP: When air frying vegetables, it's important to remove excess moisture or dab to dry the vegetables as best you can. Moisture will prevent crispy, golden crusts.

Nutritional Information

	Per Serve
Calories	156
Kilojoules	655
Total Fat	10g
– Saturated Fat	3g
Sodium	374.1mg
Carbohydrates	3.4g
– Sugar	3.4g
Fibre	5.7g
Protein	10.1g

90-Second Keto Bread
Serves 2

Yes, you read right. Now I know this isn't made in an air fryer, but likely those of you who own an air fryer will also own a microwave. I wondered if I should include this recipe, because I love it so much, and asked my staff to which the unanimous chorus chimed – YES!

- 3 tbsp. (24g) almond meal
- ½ tsp. (2g) baking powder
- 1 large egg (51g)
- 1 tbsp. (20g) melted butter (a little extra for greasing)

To make, lightly grease a mug with a little butter.

Into it whisk together the almond meal and baking powder with a pinch of sea salt.

Add the egg and melted butter and stir to combine.

Microwave for 90-seconds.

Using a long, thin knife run it around the inside edge of the mug to help release the bread.

Slice into rounds to serve.

SERVING SUGGESTION: This is just so lovely served with soup, salad, at a BBQ or lightly grilled in a hot buttered pan until golden and crispy with a poached egg.

Nutritional Information

	Per Serve
Calories	169.5
Kilojoules	712
Total Fat	15.7g
– Saturated Fat	3.9g
Sodium	238.5mg
Carbohydrates	1.4g
– Sugar	0.6g
Fibre	1.1g
Protein	5.9g

Sides

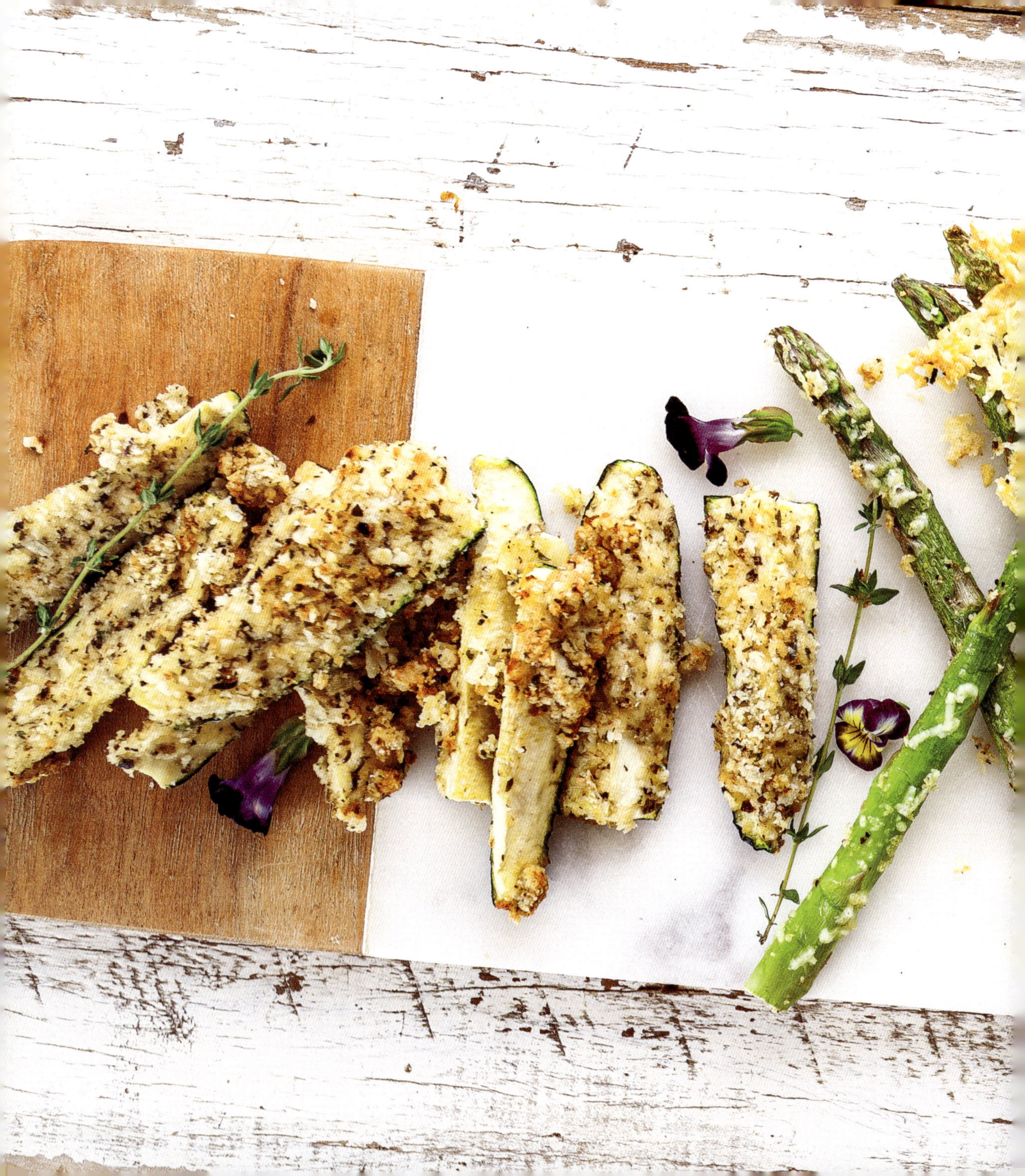

17.6g Fat
2.5g Carbs

Parmesan Zucchini Fries

Serves 4

- 2 medium zucchinis (200g each)
- 1 large egg (51g)
- ½ cup (50g) almond meal
- ½ cup (62g) grated Parmesan
- 1 tsp. (3g) fresh thyme
- 1 tbsp. (18g) olive oil

Cut zucchinis in half, then into 2cm thick, long fries.

In a bowl, whisk the egg.

On a plate, combine almond meal, Parmesan and thyme. Season and mix well.

Dredge the zucchini in the egg, then roll to coat in almond mixture, making sure all sides are well coated.

Place fries in a single layer inside the air fryer basket.

Cook at 200ºC, for 6 minutes.

Turn and cook for another 6 minutes or until golden and crispy. Repeat.

OPTIONAL: Substitute fresh thyme for taco, Cajun or garlic powder. Even dried Italian herbs, similar to the ones used in Eggplant Fries.

23.8g Fat
1.6g Carbs

Creamy Sriracha Sauce
Serves 4

This yummy dipping sauce can easily be made while the fries are cooking. Simply mix ½ cup mayonnaise + 2 tsp. each Sriracha sauce and lemon juice and season to taste.

FRIES

Eggplant Fries
Serves 4

- 1 medium eggplant (460g)
- ½ cup (50g) almond meal
- ½ cup (62g) grated Parmesan
- 1 tsp. (3g) garlic powder
- 1 tsp. (3g) dried Italian herbs
- 2 large eggs, whisked (51g each)

Cut the eggplant into strips about 2cm wide, 8 to 10cm long. Mix almond meal, Parmesan, garlic powder, Italian herbs and season. Roll the eggplant in the egg and then in the almond mixture. Cook at 180°C, for 4 minutes. Flip and cook for 3 minutes. Repeat.

14.2g Fat
4.6g Carbs

Swede Fries
Serves 4

- 2 large Swedes (700g)
- 1 tbsp. (18g) olive oil
- ½ tsp (1g) sweet paprika

Peel and slice the swede into long, thin fries then place into a large bowl. Drizzle with olive oil and toss to coat. Sprinkle generously with sweet paprika and season with sea salt and cracked pepper. Place in the air fryer basket and cook 200°C, for 6 minutes. Toss to ensure the fries are evenly exposed. Cook for another 6 minutes or until golden and cooked.

4.6g Fat
6.7g Carbs

Steak Burgers
Serves 2

A similar recipe to the Naked Cheeseburgers on p. 110, all the flavour without the calories.

- 2 rib-eye fillets, 2cm thick (200g each)
- 2 lettuce cups (15g each)
- ¼ cup (60g) grated cheddar cheese
- 2 whole pickles, sliced (25g each)
- 1 tbsp. (22g) BBQ sauce
- 1 tsp. (6g) mustard

Preheat air fryer at 180°C, for 3 minutes.

Trim any unwanted fat from room temperature meat.

Mist with oil and season with sea salt and cracked pepper.

Place streak in the air fryer basket.

Cook at 180°C, for 6 minutes. Turn and cook for another 6 minutes, for medium doneness.

Rest for 5 minutes, allowing time for the liquid to retract back into the meat; which is key for a juicy, tender steak.

Brush with BBQ sauce and mustard.

Serve in between fresh lettuce topped with cheese and pickles.

TIP: When cooking meat, remove from fridge first and allow to sit at room temperature for 20 minutes. With steaks, rub a little olive oil on both sides and season with sea salt and cracked pepper before air frying.

Nutritional Information

	Per Serve
Calories	441.1
Kilojoules	1852.6
Total Fat	21.3g
– Saturated Fat	10.4g
Sodium	628.8mg
Carbohydrates	10.3g
– Sugar	9.6g
Fibre	0.6g
Protein	51.5g

Spring Vegetable Quiche
Serves 1

This easy quiche is simple, versatile and consistently good. It's the egg custard filling that really is the most crucial part, the right ratio is required to ensure a light and fluffy result. As a general rule, its 1 egg: ½ cup milk or cream. So a 4 egg quiche: 2 cups milk, a 6 egg quiche: 3 cups milk.

- 1 large egg (51g)
- 3 tbsp. (60g) cream
- 1 tbsp. (7g) capsicum
- 1 tbsp. (8g) shallot
- 1 tbsp. (14g) corn
- 1 tbsp. (20g) cheddar cheese

Whisk together egg and cream.

Lightly grease a small 12cm ceramic quiche dish.

Distribute the chopped veggies across its base.

Pour over the egg mixture, season well and sprinkle with grated cheese.

Cook at 160ºC, for 10 minutes.

Nutritional Information

	Per Serve
Calories	363.7
Kilojoules	1527.7
Total Fat	33g
– Saturated Fat	19.6g
Sodium	267.2mg
Carbohydrates	3.9g
– Sugar	2.8g
Fibre	0.9g
Protein	13.2g

Pork Mince Patties

Makes 4

I haven't added it in this recipe, but my Nana used to always add a teaspoon of chicken stock to her pork rissoles for extra flavour.

- 2 cloves garlic, crushed (6g)
- 500g pork mince
- 1 spring onion, chopped (15g)
- 1 carrot, grated (120g)
- ¼ cup fresh coriander (10g)
- 1 large egg (51g)

In a bowl, place all ingredients and season well.

Mix to combine.

Roll into 4 equal patties.

Place into air fryer basket and cook for 4 minutes.

Turn and cook for an additional 3 to 4 minutes or until done.

Remove the patties from the air fryer and enjoy immediately or refrigerate for up to 3 days.

OPTIONAL: I added some marinated capsicum simply because I had them.

Nutritional Information

	Per Serve
Calories	248.6
Kilojoules	1044.1
Total Fat	14.5g
– Saturated Fat	5.3g
Sodium	108.1mg
Carbohydrates	2.7g
– Sugar	2.3g
Fibre	1.6g
Protein	26.5g

Mustard Wings
Serves 4

Fresh chicken wings cook very fast in the air fryer. Whatever wings you are cooking, the simple way to do so is to place the chicken wings in the air fryer basket with space between and cook at 200°C, for 12 minutes. Shake or flip the wings and cook for another 12 minutes or until crispy.

- 1kg chicken wings
- ½ cup (146g) yellow mustard
- 1 tsp. (6g) sea salt
- ½ tsp. (3g) cracked pepper

Preheat air fryer at 180°C, for 3 minutes.

Remove excess moisture from chicken wings with absorbent paper.

Place wings in a large bowl and toss with mustard to fully coat.

Season well with sea salt and cracked pepper.

Place wings into the air fryer basket.

Cook at 180°C, for 30 minutes, shaking the basket every 10 minutes to ensure the wings cook evenly all over.

Remove when the wings are crisped to your liking.

Honey Mustard Wings
Serves 4

45.4g Fat
19.5g Carbs

Although honey isn't KETO, this recipe was just delicious, so we decided to add it anyway.

In a bowl mix 2 tsp. baking powder and 1 tsp. sea salt. Toss 500g chicken wings through it. Place in air fryer basket. Cook at 200°C, for 10 minutes.

Mix ¼ cup honey and ¼ cup Dijon mustard, season with sea salt and cracked pepper. Brush across the wings, totally coating. Cook at 200°C, for 10 minutes more.

Nutritional Information

	Per Serve
Calories	578.5
Kilojoules	2429.7
Total Fat	44.7g
– Saturated Fat	13.4g
Sodium	1215.2mg
Carbohydrates	2.6g
– Sugar	1.3g
Fibre	1.7g
Protein	42.4g

Air Fryer Stuffed Mushrooms
Serves 4

- 16 large mushrooms (560g), stalks removed
- 1 tbsp. (20g) butter
- 2 cloves garlic, crushed (6g)
- ½ small onion, diced (60g)
- 125g cream cheese, softened
- ¼ tsp. (1g) thyme leaves
- 1 tsp. (6g) Worcestershire sauce
- 1 tbsp. (5g) fresh parsley, chopped
- ¼ cup (30g) grated Parmesan

In a non-stick frying pan over a medium heat melt the butter, sauté onion for 5 minutes.

Add crushed garlic and stir until fragrant, 2 to 3 minutes.

Set aside to cool.

In a bowl combine remaining ingredients.

Add sautéed onions.

Stir to combine.

Fill each mushroom and season.

Place in an air fryer basket (may need to cook in two batches, depending on the size of the air fryer and mushrooms).

Cook at 180ºC, for 8 minutes or until golden.

Serve immediately.

Nutritional Information

	Per Serve
Calories	186.5
Kilojoules	783.3
Total Fat	14.9g
– Saturated Fat	8.6g
Sodium	253.9mg
Carbohydrates	1.3g
– Sugar	1.2g
Fibre	2.7g
Protein	9.1g

Mushroom Parmigiana
Makes 4

- 4 large Portobello mushrooms (300g), stems removed
- ¼ cup (70g) pizza paste
- 4 rounds champagne ham (12g each)
- ½ cup (60g) grated 3-cheese mix

Spread pizza paste across each mushroom (gill side up).

Lay across a round of ham and top with grated cheese.

Season.

Place into air fryer basket, cook at 180ºC, for 10 to 12 minutes or until cheese is golden

Nutritional Information

	Per Serve
Calories	89
Kilojoules	373.8
Total Fat	4.1g
– Saturated Fat	2.5g
Sodium	410.2mg
Carbohydrates	3.6g
– Sugar	2.6g
Fibre	1.9g
Protein	7.6g

Lamb Kebabs
Serves 6

- 1 lemon, juiced (80ml)
- 2 tbsp. (36g) olive oil
- 1 tbsp. (5g) finely chopped rosemary (or dried oregano)
- 2 garlic cloves, crushed (6g)
- 1kg lamb leg steaks, cut into 2.5cm pieces

In a large bowl, combine the lemon juice, oil, rosemary and garlic. Season.

Add lamb and stir to coat.

Cover and refrigerate for at least 30 minutes to marinate (the longer the better).

Remove from fridge 20 minutes prior to cooking.

Thread 5 or 6 pieces of lamb on each.

Cook at 180ºC, for 15 minutes, turning halfway.

Once done, sit for 2 minutes, as they will continue to cook in the residual heat.

8.7g Fat
1.4g Carbs

Lamb Mint Rissoles
Serves 4

- 1 small red onion, finely diced (118g)
- 2 tbsp. (10g) fresh mint, chopped
- ½ tsp. (1.5g) curry powder

Line the air fryer basket with baking paper. In a bowl, combine all ingredients and season with sea salt and cracked pepper

Roll into 4 equal patties. Place in the air fryer basket. Cook at 180ºC, for 8 minutes. Using tongs, flip and cook for another 8 minutes.

Nutritional Information

	Per Serve
Calories	284.2
Kilojoules	1193.7
Total Fat	15.5g
– Saturated Fat	4.3g
Sodium	88.5mg
Carbohydrates	0.4g
– Sugar	0.3g
Fibre	0.6g
Protein	35.5g

Keto Chicken Tenders
Serves 4

Kids love them, fast food restaurants count on them and advertisers use them to lure in millions of hungry diners each year. When it comes to takeaway, chicken tenders reign supreme.

- 500g chicken tenderloins
- 1 large egg (51g)
- ½ cup (50g) almond meal
- ½ cup (62g) grated Parmesan
- ½ tsp. (1g) Cajun seasoning
- 1 tbsp. (18g) olive oil spray

In a large bowl, beat the egg.

Onto a dinner plate mix together the almond meal, cheese and seasoning.

Season with sea salt and cracked pepper; mix to combine.

Dip each tender in egg, then roll in almond mixture.

Roll again, to ensure the tenders are well covered.

Place in the air fryer basket.

Lightly mist with olive oil.

Cook at 180ºC, for 10 minutes.

Turn and cook at 200ºC, for 3 minutes to brown the crust.

Keto Ketchup
Makes ½ cup

0.1g Fat
4.3g Carbs

In a small saucepan mix ½ cup tomato paste, ¼ cup Natvia, 3 tbsp. white wine vinegar, 1 tsp. onion powered and ½ tsp. garlic powder with 1 cup water. Season with sea salt. Simmer over a low heat for 30 minutes or until thickened to your liking. Season to taste.

Nutritional Information

	Per Serve
Calories	328.6
Kilojoules	1380.2
Total Fat	19.3g
– Saturated Fat	4.9g
Sodium	363.1mg
Carbohydrates	0.9g
– Sugar	0.5g
Fibre	1.2g
Protein	37.6g

Eggplant Pizza
Serves 2

An air fryer works like a convection style oven. It circulates hot air around a metal basket which creates a crispy outer layer. Not to get all scientific here but there is something called the 'Maillard' reaction, which is the chemical reaction that gives food a browned or crispy crust. An air fryer makes that reaction happen, and works particularly well with eggplant once its moisture has been removed.

- 1 large eggplant (459g)
- ½ cup (138g) pizza paste
- 2 garlic cloves, crushed (6g)
- ¾ cup (90g) shredded mozzarella cheese
- 6 cherry tomatoes (48g)
- 2 small yellow capsicums, sliced (65g)

Slice the eggplant lengthwise, about 1.5cm thick.

Rub some salt on both sides of the slices and rest on absorbent paper for at least 10 to 15 minutes. Doing this allows the water to leach out from the inner cells, making the eggplant soft when cooked. Dab dry.

Sprinkle with sea salt and pepper.

Place in the air fryer basket and cook at 180ºC, for 5 minutes.

Meanwhile, mix together pizza paste and minced garlic.

Spread the pizza mix across the top of each eggplant slice.

Sprinkle with mozzarella, cherry tomatoes and capsicum rounds.

Season with sea salt and cracked pepper.

Cook at 180ºC, for 6 minutes or until golden brown.

Nutritional Information

	Per Serve
Calories	274.7
Kilojoules	1153.7
Total Fat	11.9g
– Saturated Fat	7.8g
Sodium	903.1mg
Carbohydrates	21.8g
– Sugar	18g
Fibre	9.5g
Protein	17.2g

Coconut Prawns
Serves 4

Made in the air fryer, these healthy coconut prawns are nice and crunchy yet made without the need for a lot of oil. It's so quick and easy to cook prawns in the air fryer and this recipe is one of our favourites.

- 2 large eggs (51g each)
- ½ cup (50g) almond meal
- ½ tsp. (1g) onion powder
- ½ tsp. (1g) garlic powder
- ½ tsp. (1g) sweet paprika
- 1¼ cups (112g) shredded coconut
- 12 king prawns, peeled and de-veined, tail on (228g)

In one bowl, whisk the eggs.

In another bowl, combine all dry ingredients.

Dredge each prawn in egg wash, then coat in the coconut mixture making sure it's totally covered.

Place prawns in the air fryer basket and cook at 180ºC, for 5 minutes. Turn and cook for another 3 minutes or until done.

TIP: Pat the prawns dry before coating. This will help the prawns get really crispy, if there is excess moisture the air fryer prawns can steam and become soggy.

Spicy Mayo
Serves 4

18.7g Fat
7g Carbs

This spicy dipping sauce goes perfectly with the sweet coconut prawns.

In a small bowl, combine:
- ½ cup (120g) mayonnaise
- 1 tbsp. (10g) Sriracha sauce
- 1 tbsp. (28g) sweet chilli sauce

Nutritional Information

	Per Serve
Calories	349.1
Kilojoules	1466.4
Total Fat	28.1g
– Saturated Fat	17.4g
Sodium	240.4mg
Carbohydrates	3.1g
– Sugar	2.6g
Fibre	5.6g
Protein	19.5g

Baked Avocado with Salmon
Serves 4

- 2 tbsp. (22g) finely chopped red onion
- 4 tbsp. (80g) cream cheese
- 1 tbsp. (11g) capers
- 100g smoked salmon

- 2 avocados (216g each), cut in half, stone removed

Preheat air fryer at 180°C, for 3 minutes.

In a small bowl, combine onion, cream cheese and capers and season with cracked pepper.

Spoon the mixture across each of the avocado cups and place in the air fryer basket.

Cook at 180°C, for 6 minutes.

Transfer to serving plates.

Top with smoked salmon.

OPTIONAL: Serve garnished with fresh dill and a splash of lemon juice.

Nutritional Information

	Per Serve
Calories	255.6
Kilojoules	1073.5
Total Fat	22.4g
– Saturated Fat	6.2g
Sodium	422.3mg
Carbohydrates	0.7g
– Sugar	0.4g
Fibre	8.3g
Protein	9.7g

Antipasto Kebabs
Makes 12

These are just delicious – sweet, salty, juicy – moreish!

- 12 pitted Kalamata olives (48g)
- 180g haloumi, cubed
- 12 rounds Hungarian salami (276g), folded
- 12 rounds sopressa (276g), folded
- 12 cherry tomatoes (96g)
- 12 capsicum squares (224g) (green, red or both)

Onto each skewer place one of each of the above ingredients.

Pop each skewer into the air fryer.

Cook at 160ºC, for 5 minutes.

Turn and cook again for 4 minutes.

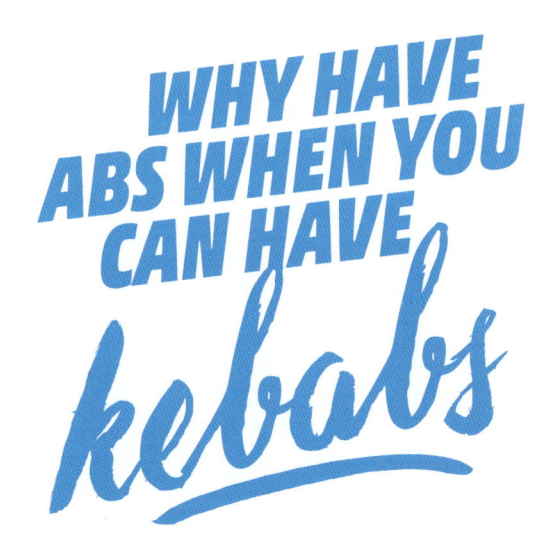

WHY HAVE ABS WHEN YOU CAN HAVE kebabs

Nutritional Information

	Per Serve
Calories	236.2
Kilojoules	992
Total Fat	19.2g
– Saturated Fat	7.3g
Sodium	1222.7mg
Carbohydrates	2.3g
– Sugar	1.5g
Fibre	0.6g
Protein	13.5g

Lunch

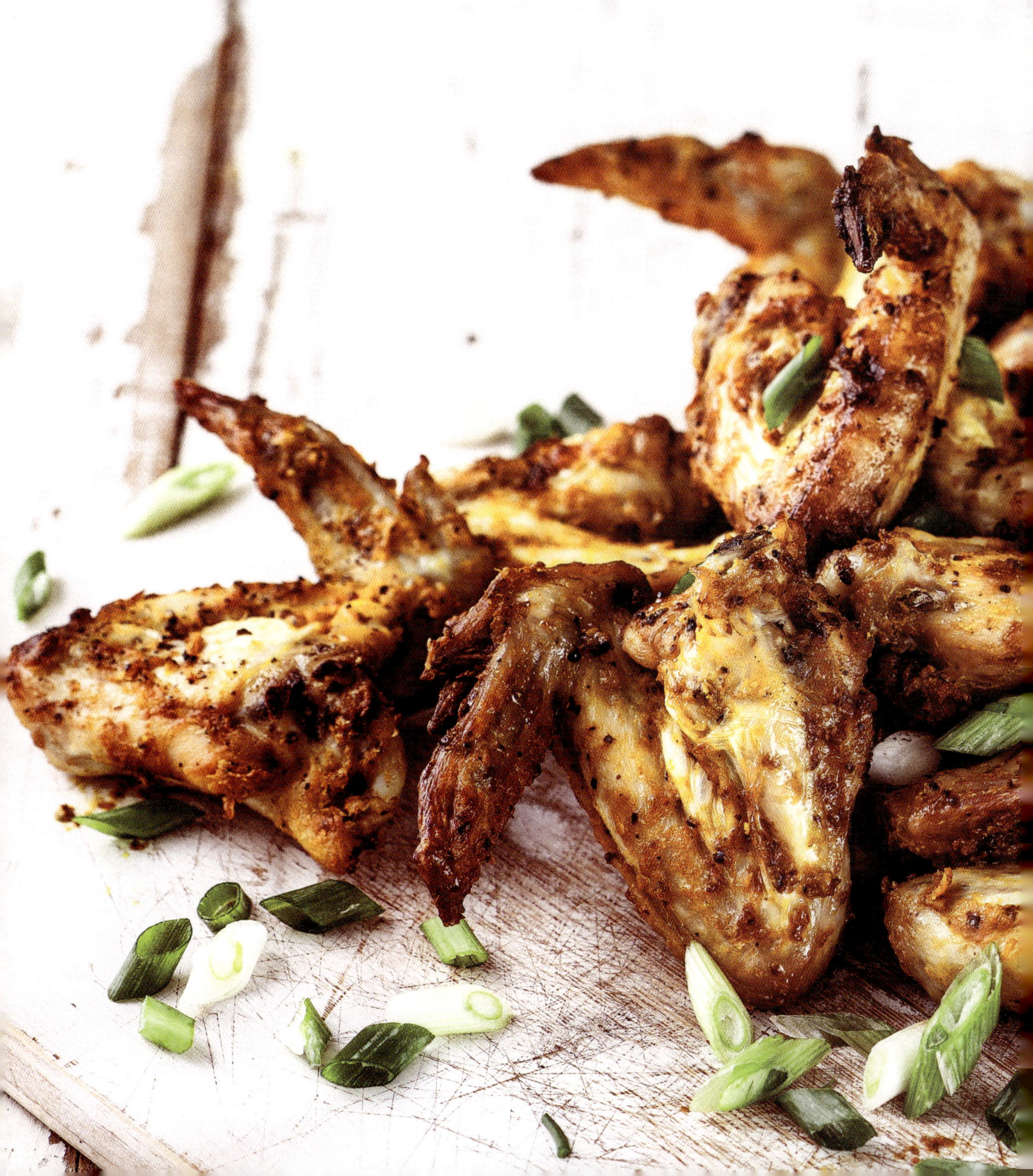

Sweet Jalapeño Poppers
Makes 16

I am yet to make these for anyone who doesn't enjoy them – sweet popping poppers – pass me another please!

- 8 whole jalapeños (400g)
- 150g cream cheese, softened
- ½ cup (60g) grated cheddar cheese
- ¼ cup (26g) chopped shallot
- ¼ cup (66g) ranch dressing
- 4 slices (70g) prosciutto, cut into long strips

Cut each jalapeño in half.

Remove the seeds and membrane.

In a bowl, mix together the cream cheese, cheddar, shallot and ranch dressing.

Season to taste.

Stuff each half with the cream cheese and wrap with prosciutto.

Cook at 180ºC, for 10 to 12 minutes or until the jalapeños are tender and the prosciutto golden and crisp.

Enjoy!

Nutritional Information

	Per Serve
Calories	78.6
Kilojoules	330
Total Fat	6.7g
– Saturated Fat	2.9g
Sodium	178mg
Carbohydrates	0.9g
– Sugar	0.9g
Fibre	0.6g
Protein	3.5g

Steak & Mushroom Bites
Serves 4

My boys absolutely love these; easy to make and even easier to eat.

- 500g rib-eye fillet steak
- 2 tbsp. (50g) Worcestershire sauce
- 1 clove garlic, crushed
- 20 button mushrooms (400g)

Cut the steak into 20 bite size pieces.

Sprinkle generously with a ¾ teaspoon of sea salt and pepper.

Add Worcestershire and garlic and marinate for 1 hour.

In the final 15 minutes add the mushrooms and toss to coat.

Place the steak and mushrooms into the air fryer basket.

Cook at 180ºC, for 5 minutes.

Shake well and cook for 5 minutes more.

To serve simply thread one mushroom onto a toothpick followed by a piece of steak.

STEAK makes me HAPPY

Nutritional Information

	Per Serve
Calories	211.4
Kilojoules	888
Total Fat	8.4g
– Saturated Fat	3.1g
Sodium	208.8mg
Carbohydrates	2.2g
– Sugar	2.1g
Fibre	1.5g
Protein	30g

Prosciutto Wrapped Brie

Serves 4

Is there anything better than melted cheese? Warm and gooey, it is a crowd favourite. Here's another of my personal favourites. Pop a round of brie into a baking dish. Top with chopped walnuts, dried cherries or cranberries and finely diced rosemary. Season and drizzle with honey. Cook at 160ºC, for 10 minutes. Similarly, a round of camembert topped with chilli flakes, rosemary and honey. Season. Cook at 160ºC, for 10 minutes.

- 250g double brie cheese wheel
- 115g prosciutto, thinly sliced

Line the air fryer basket with baking paper.

Lay 4 slices of prosciutto onto a dry, clean surface, overlapping so they form a sheet.

Place brie in the centre and fold the prosciutto over it to enclose.

Place in the air fryer, seam side down.

Cook at 160ºC, for 10 minutes or until the prosciutto is nice and crisp.

Carefully remove to a platter or plate.

OPTIONAL: If you don't mind the extra carbs, add 2 tablespoons of your favourite chutney or jam to the top of the Brie before wrapping.

SERVING SUGGESTION: Enjoy this with low-carb crackers, crunchy baguette, or just dig straight in with a fork.

Nutritional Information

	Per Serve
Calories	329.9
Kilojoules	1385.6
Total Fat	26.5g
– Saturated Fat	15.2g
Sodium	950mg
Carbohydrates	0.8g
– Sugar	0.8g
Fibre	0g
Protein	23.9g

Parmesan Crusted Olives
Serves 4

Olive Me LOVES Olive You!

- ½ cup (50g) almond meal
- ⅓ cup (41g) Parmesan
- 24 marinated feta stuffed green olives (100g)

Line the air fryer basket with baking paper.

In a bowl, mix together the almond meal and Parmesan.

Remove olives from oil, roll in almond and Parmesan mix, then place into the air fryer basket.

Repeat.

Cook at 160ºC, for 8 minutes shaking half way through.

Serve immediately.

Sweet & Smokey Roasted Almonds
Serves 4

16.7g Fat
1.2g Carbs

In an oven-proof bowl, add 1 cup of almonds and lightly spray with oil, tossing to coat. In a small bowl mix together 1 tsp. each of Natvia, sea salt, smoky paprika with ½ tsp. ground cinnamon. Sprinkle over the almonds, again tossing to coat.

Place the bowl in the air fryer basket. Cook at 160ºC, for 5 minutes. Shake and cook for another 5 minutes.

Nutritional Information

	Per Serve
Calories	165
Kilojoules	692.8
Total Fat	14.8g
– Saturated Fat	3.1g
Sodium	415.5mg
Carbohydrates	0.9g
– Sugar	0.6g
Fibre	1.8g
Protein	6.9g

Jalapeño Cheesy Bread
Makes 6

- 1 cup (120g) grated cheese (cheddar or mozzarella)
- ½ cup (60g) grated Parmesan
- 2 large eggs (51g each)
- ¼ cup (40g) pickled jalapeños, diced

Line the air fryer basket with baking paper.

Combine the ingredients in a bowl and season.

Mix well to combine.

Roughly divide the mixture into six equal parts, and dollop onto the baking paper.

Cook at 180°C, for 8 minutes.

Gently flip and cook for another 4 minutes or until the cheese has melted and created a crispy brown crust.

OPTIONAL: Add a whole jalapeño to the top before baking if you like extra bite.

12.3g Fat
0.3g Carbs

3-Ingredient Cheesy Breadsticks
Serves 4

Line the air fryer basket with baking paper. In a bowl mix together 1½ cup (180g) grated mozzarella cheese, 2 eggs (51g each) and ½ tsp. (1.3g) Italian seasoning. Spread the mixture across the base of the air fryer and season with sea salt and cracked pepper. Cook at 180°C, for 10 minutes. Cool for 5 minutes before slicing into 'sticks' to serve.

Nutritional Information

	Per Serve
Calories	139.7
Kilojoules	586.5
Total Fat	10.2g
– Saturated Fat	6.1g
Sodium	392.7mg
Carbohydrates	1.2g
– Sugar	1.1g
Fibre	0.1g
Protein	10.6g

Salsa Topped Haloumi Wedges
Serves 4

Grilled haloumi: it's trendy, it's easy and it's quick, but the real reason to try grilled haloumi – IT'S DELICIOUS!

- 100g marinated, roasted capsicum, chopped (reserve a little oil)
- 1 vine-ripened tomato, seeded and chopped (138g)
- 6 Kalamata olives, chopped (24g)
- 6 basil leaves, roughly chopped (5g)
- 300g block haloumi cheese

Combine capsicum, tomato, olives and basil and a teaspoon of reserved oil in a small bowl. Season to taste and set aside.

Slice the block of haloumi into quarters, then each quarter in half creating 8 wedges.

Brush each with the reserved oil and place in the air fryer.

Cook at 180ºC, for 5 minutes. Flip and cook another 2 minutes or until golden.

Serve piled high with the yummy heart-healthy salsa.

NEW YEAR Hallou NEW ME

Nutritional Information

	Per Serve
Calories	218.2
Kilojoules	916.5
Total Fat	14.2g
– Saturated Fat	8.6g
Sodium	2323.7mg
Carbohydrates	5g
– Sugar	4.1g
Fibre	1g
Protein	16.6g

Crispy Salami Roll-Ups
Makes 12

NOW THESE ARE GOOD – cream cheese and salty salami are a stellar combination. Add whatever you want to the filling; semi-dried tomatoes, chopped olives and fresh herbs are all lovely.

- 250g cream cheese
- 2 tbsp. (23g) capers, drained and chopped
- 1 tbsp. (5g) finely chopped basil
- 12 rounds Hungarian salami (276g)

In a small bowl mix together cream cheese, capers and basil.

Season with cracked pepper.

Lay the salami onto a clean surface and spread a generous tablespoon of mixture across each.

Roll up across itself and place seam side down into the air fryer basket.

Cook at 180ºC, for 7 minutes.

lil bit SALTY

Nutritional Information

	Per Serve
Calories	157.6
Kilojoules	661.8
Total Fat	14.4g
– Saturated Fat	6.5g
Sodium	528.5mg
Carbohydrates	0.4g
– Sugar	0.2g
Fibre	0.1g
Protein	6.8g

Chorizo Chips
Serves 4

Chorizo – POR-FAVOR!

- 225g spicy cured chorizo sausage, sliced into 4mm thick rounds
- 1 tsp. (1g) chopped rosemary
- ½ tsp. (0.5g) fresh thyme leaves

Preheat air fryer at 180ºC, for 3 minutes.

Slice the chorizo into 4mm thick rounds.

Sprinkle with fresh rosemary and thyme and season with cracked pepper.

Cook at 180ºC, for 3 minutes.

Shake and cook again for 2 minutes.

Serve immediately.

SERVING SUGGESTIONS: These are a wonderful addition to any platter or grazing board.

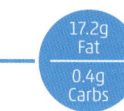

Salami Crisps
Serves 4

17.2g Fat
0.4g Carbs

These salami chips are so easy. Keto doesn't get any simpler!

Place 8 rounds of salami in the air fryer basket, limiting how much they overlap. Cook at 180ºC, for 2 minutes, turn and cook for another 2 minutes.

Remove to absorbent paper. Serve warm with your favourite cheese and fresh vegetable sticks.

Nutritional Information

	Per Serve
Calories	159.5
Kilojoules	670.1
Total Fat	12.5g
– Saturated Fat	4.5g
Sodium	619mg
Carbohydrates	0.8g
– Sugar	0.5g
Fibre	0.4g
Protein	11.3g

Baked Feta
Serves 4

By now, you have seen this recipe doing the rounds on social media; there's just something about that salty, creamy, cheesy combination that appeals to us all. This is our take on it done in the air fryer and... it's every bit as nice as it is roasted!

- 1 tbsp. (18g) olive oil
- 200g feta cheese
- 250g punnet cherry tomatoes
- 2 yellow mini-capsicums, chopped (65g)
- 1 garlic clove, crushed (3g)

Brush a 10cm air fryer safe dish with oil.

Place the feta in it.

Nestle tomatoes and capsicums around it.

Mix together remaining olive oil and garlic and drizzle.

Season well with sea salt and cracked pepper.

Cook at 160ºC, for 10 minutes or until nice and golden.

Carefully remove.

OPTIONAL: Sprinkle with fresh thyme and rosemary if you have them.

SERVING SUGGESTION: Serve with your favourite Keto crackers and a mezze of fresh vegetable rounds.

Nutritional Information

	Per Serve
Calories	194.9
Kilojoules	818.4
Total Fat	16.4g
– Saturated Fat	8.4g
Sodium	541.6mg
Carbohydrates	2.2g
– Sugar	2.2g
Fibre	1.5g
Protein	9.6g

Avocado Wafers
Makes 10

Ideally you will have a larger air fryer with trays to make these. If not, you may prefer to bake them in your oven. Same preparation, just bake in a 160°C oven for 15 minutes, gently flip and bake for 2 minutes more.

- 1 large, ripe avocado (216g)
- ¾ cup (93g) grated Parmesan
- 1 tsp. (5ml) lemon juice
- ½ tsp. (1.3g) garlic powder
- ¼ tsp. (0.7g) onion powder

In a bowl, mash the avocado until creamy.

Add remaining ingredients and season with cracked pepper.

Line each tray with baking paper.

Onto each, spread thinly the mixture forming nice round circles.

Bake at 180°C, for 8 minutes.

Cool for 1 minute before gently flipping; rotate higher tray to lower position (as heat rises) and cook for another 5 minutes or until all golden.

Note: These yummy wafers will crisp as they cool.

Asparagus Wrapped Prosciutto
Serves 6

3.3g Fat
0.7g Carbs

- 18 fresh asparagus
- 6 slices prosciutto

Trim the asparagus by simply snapping it. The asparagus will naturally snap where the woody end starts. Slice each piece of prosciutto into long thin strips, depending on the width, you may cut 3-4 strips from each. Roll each strip around the spear. Place in the air fryer basket. Cook at 180°C, for 7 minutes. Serve with a light splash of balsamic glaze.

Nutritional Information

	Per Serve
Calories	67.9
Kilojoules	285.1
Total Fat	5.6g
– Saturated Fat	2.1g
Sodium	123.4mg
Carbohydrates	0.1g
– Sugar	0.1g
Fibre	1.7g
Protein	3.7g

Snacks

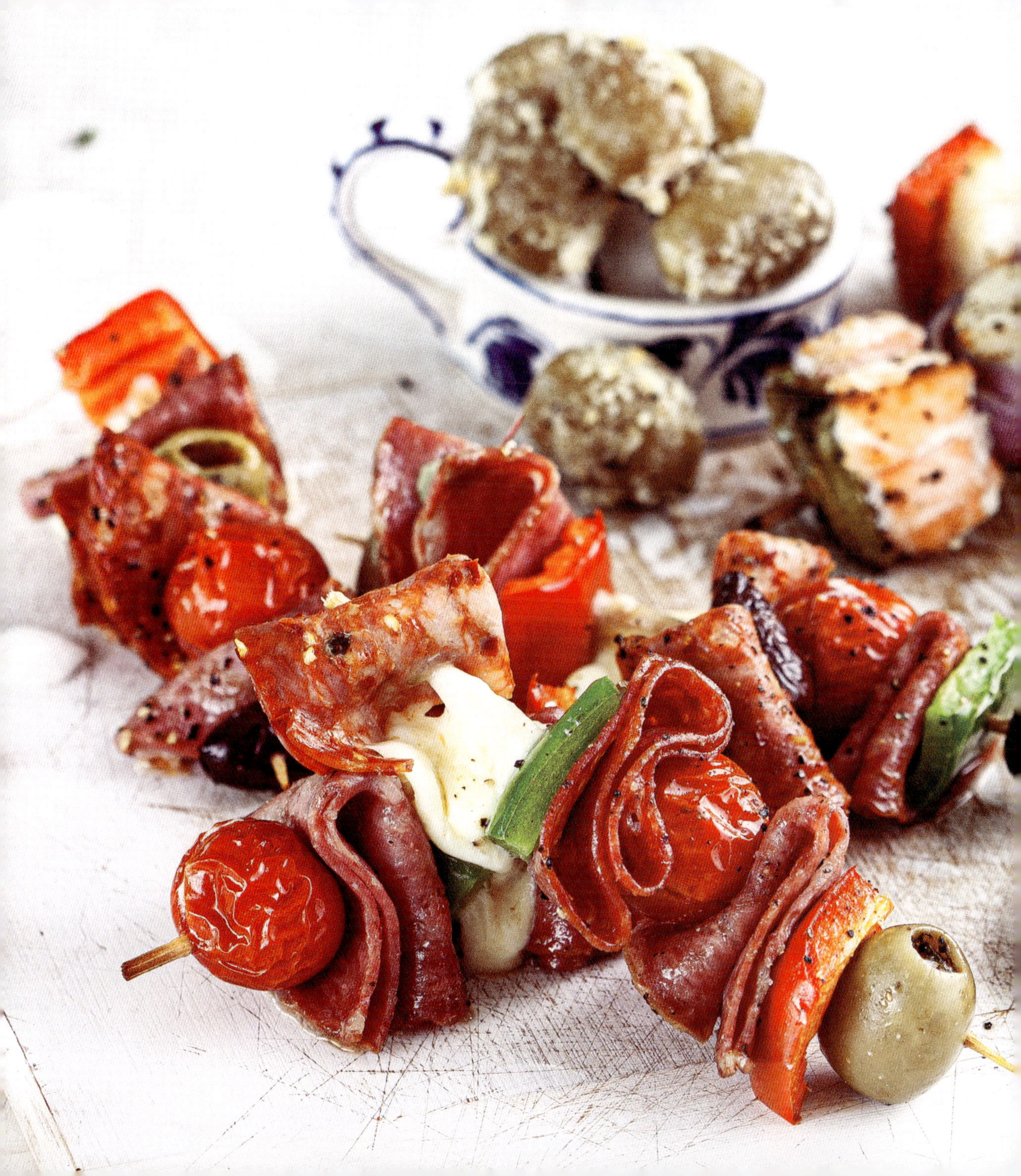

Smashed Avo on Cauliflower Hash Browns
Serves 2

- 350g frozen cauliflower rice, thawed
- 1 large egg (51g), whisked
- ½ cup (60g) grated mozzarella cheese
- 1 large, ripe avocado (216g)
- ½ tsp. (1.3g) garlic powder

Line the air fryer basket with baking paper.

Squeeze excess moisture from the cauliflower.

Pat dry before placing in a large bowl.

Add egg and mozzarella and season, stir well.

Divide the mixture into 4 and spoon into rounds on the baking paper.

Cook at 200ºC, for 5 minutes.

Gently flip and cook for another 4 minutes.

Meanwhile, into a bowl, place avocado and garlic powder and season.

Mix well until nice and creamy.

To serve, spread across cauliflower toasts and serve immediately.

SERVING SUGGESTION: Sprinkle lightly with chilli flakes.

21.3g Fat
1.4g Carbs

Broccoli Smashed Hash Browns
Serves 2

Take 350g frozen broccoli rice, thaw and squeeze as much liquid as possible from it. Pat dry with absorbent paper.

In a bowl, mix together broccoli rice, ½ cup (60g) grated cheddar cheese, 1 large egg (51g) and 2 tbsp. (16g) almond meal. Season.

Line air fryer basket with baking paper. Place 6 equal rounds in air fryer basket and gently press to flatten. Cook at 200ºC, for 5 minutes. Flip and cook for another 4 minutes. Repeat.

Nutritional Information

	Per Serve
Calories	338.4
Kilojoules	1421.2
Total Fat	27.6g
– Saturated Fat	11g
Sodium	395.6mg
Carbohydrates	4.7g
– Sugar	3.8g
Fibre	9.8g
Protein	14.7g

Keto Bagels
Makes 4

Bagels are a dense type of bread, shaped like a donut that lends itself to different flavours and fillings. A Keto bagel is even denser than usual with almond and cheese the main ingredients – dense but delicious!

- 1 cup (100g) almond meal
- ½ tsp. (2.3g) baking powder
- ¼ cup (75g) shredded mozzarella
- 1 tbsp. (20g) cream cheese
- 1 large egg (51g)

Preheat air fryer at 180ºC, for 3 minutes.

Mix the almond meal and baking powder together. Season with a pinch of salt.

Melt the mozzarella and cream cheese in a bowl in the microwave for 30 seconds.

Cool, then add the egg. Stir to combine.

Add the almond meal and knead into a dough.

Divide into 4 even portions, roll into sausages, 8cm long.

Pinch the ends together to make a donut shape.

Place on baking paper.

Bake at 160ºC, for 10 minutes.

Remove and Enjoy!

OPTIONAL: Lightly mist with olive oil spray and sprinkle with sesame seeds.

SERVING SUGGESTION: For a delicious savoury bagel, spread with cream cheese, top with smoked salmon and fresh dill. For a delicious sweet bagel, spread with nut butter of choice and sliced strawberries – or – sour cream, Natvia and fresh mixed berries.

Nutritional Information

	Per Serve
Calories	222.7
Kilojoules	935.5
Total Fat	19.4g
– Saturated Fat	4.4g
Sodium	196.4mg
Carbohydrates	1.6g
– Sugar	1g
Fibre	2.2g
Protein	10g

Ham & Egg Cup
Serves 1

Ham and eggs are like peas and carrots. Whether you are eating them for breakfast or as part of a casserole for dinner, hot or cold, baked or scrambled, we all LOVE ham and eggs!

- 25g round ham off the bone
- 1 large egg (51g)
- 1 tbsp. (20g) cream
- 1 tbsp. (20g) cheddar cheese
- 1 cherry tomato (8g)

Gently press a large round of ham into a ramekin.

In a small bowl, whisk together egg and cream; pour into ham.

Sprinkle with cheese and top with a cherry tomato.

Season.

Cook at 180ºC, 6 minutes for a single egg, 7 for a double.

OPTIONAL: Sprinkle with freshly chopped chives before baking. Serve with a drizzle of Worcestershire Sauce.

26.6g Fat
4.6g Carbs

Breakfast Sausages
Serves 1

Preheat air fryer at 180ºC, for 3 minutes.

Place 4 chipolata sausages (140g) in air fryer basket. Cook at 180ºC, for 8 minutes shaking half way through. Check for doneness (may need a couple more minutes).

Nutritional Information

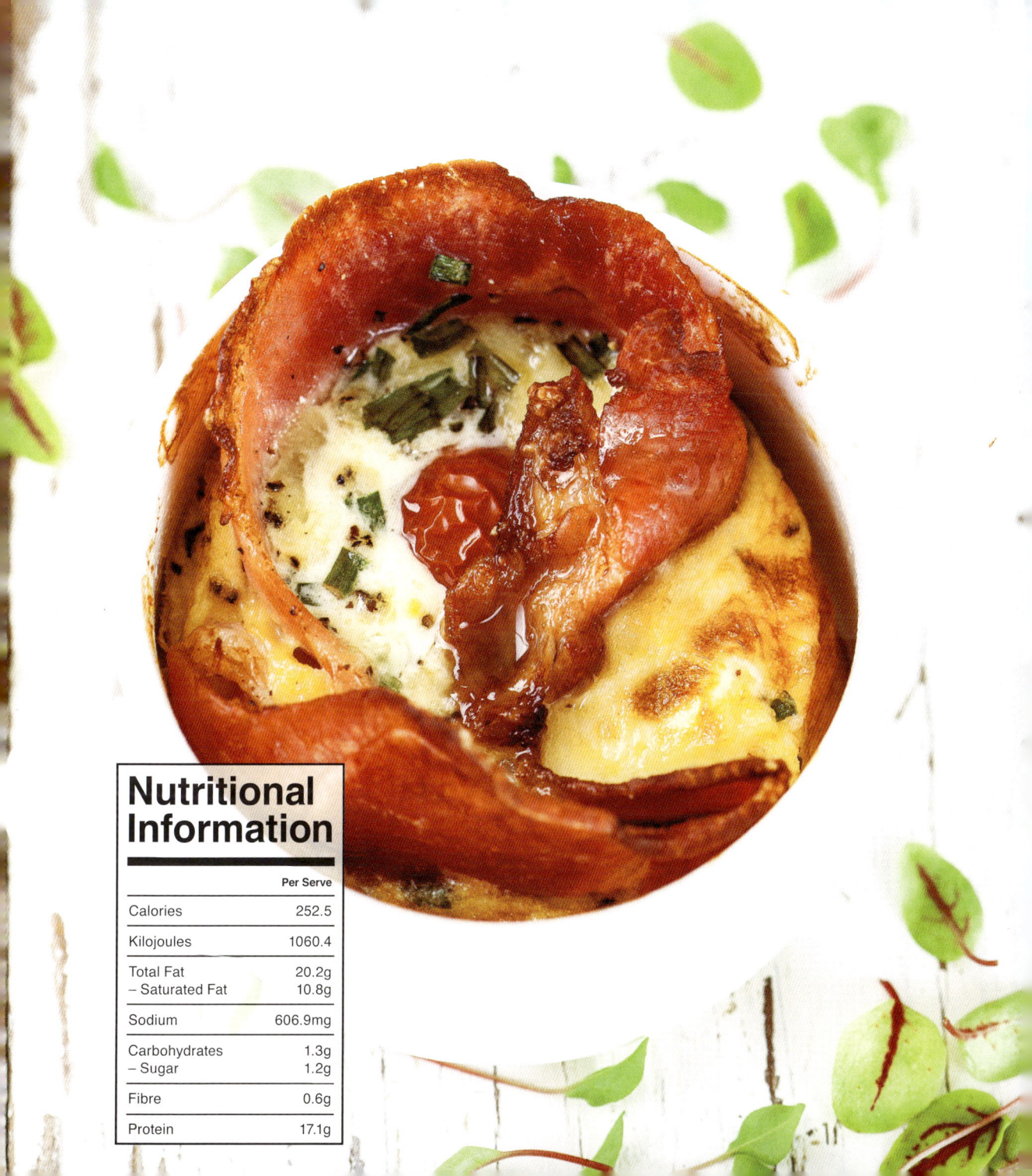

	Per Serve
Calories	252.5
Kilojoules	1060.4
Total Fat	20.2g
– Saturated Fat	10.8g
Sodium	606.9mg
Carbohydrates	1.3g
– Sugar	1.2g
Fibre	0.6g
Protein	17.1g

Easy Homemade Granola
Makes 4

This granola has got taste and texture, the air fryer evenly browns the ingredients and makes them all perfectly crunchy. Serve with your favourite yoghurt and fresh berries for a fibre-rich start to your day.

- 2 cups (220g) pecan nuts, chopped
- 1 cup (85g) coconut flakes
- 1 cup (122g) slivered almonds
- 1 tsp. (2.6g) cinnamon
- 1 tbsp. (18g) coconut oil spray

In a large bowl, mix the pecans, coconut flakes, slivered almonds and ground cinnamon.

Lightly mist with coconut oil spray, toss and lightly mist again.

Line the air fryer basket with baking paper.

Pour the mixture into the basket.

Cook at 160ºC, for 4 minutes, toss and cook 3 minutes more.

STORING SUGGESTION: Store in airtight container at room temperature up to 5 days.

EAT BREAKFAST THEN change the world

Nutritional Information

	Per Serve
Calories	357.4
Kilojoules	1500.8
Total Fat	33.5g
– Saturated Fat	6.4g
Sodium	30.2mg
Carbohydrates	6.8g
– Sugar	5.8g
Fibre	4.6g
Protein	6.4g

Baked Avocado Eggs
Serves 2

Not only are they easy to prepare but they are packed full of everything you can possibly need for a healthy sustainable breakfast. This recipe is not a new one, in fact, it's been around for ages – but it's here again – just add your favourite seasonings!

- 1 avocado (216g), cut in half, stone removed
- 2 large eggs (51g each)
- 1 tbsp. (5g) chopped chives

Line the air fryer basket with baking paper.

Place avocado halves into air fryer basket.

Crack an egg into each (you may need to scoop out some of the filling if you don't think the egg will fit snugly), season and sprinkle with chives.

Cook at 180ºC, 5 minutes for a soft runny egg, 6 to 7 minutes for a harder egg.

SERVING SUGGESTIONS: Serve sprinkled with sweet paprika, or fresh lime zest or drizzled with a deliciously tangy Hollandaise Sauce.

Hollandaise Sauce
Serves 2

45.2g Fat
0.4g Carbs

- 2 large egg yolks (16g each)
- 100g butter
- 2 tbsp. (40ml) lemon juice

In a bowl whisk the egg yolks. In a small saucepan over a low heat, melt the butter. Add the lemon juice and season with sea salt and cracked pepper. Gradually add the egg, whisking all the time to incorporate. Serve immediately.

Nutritional Information

	Per Serve
Calories	218.6
Kilojoules	918
Total Fat	19g
– Saturated Fat	3.4g
Sodium	80.2mg
Carbohydrates	0.5g
– Sugar	0.2g
Fibre	8.2g
Protein	8.4g

Bacon & Egg Bites
Serves 2

There is no denying the chemistry between bacon and eggs. It's literally that good you can add any number of nutrient-dense veggies to them and still they are the primary flavours. Starting each day with a protein rich breakfast is just clever – this recipe is not only smart but easy too.

- 3 large eggs (51g each)
- 2 tbsp. (40g) cream
- 1 tbsp. (7g) chopped red capsicum
- 1 tbsp. (11g) finely chopped red onion
- 1 tbsp. (3.6g) finely chopped spinach
- 1 tbsp. (20g) grated cheddar cheese
- 2 tbsp. (50g) crumbled bacon

Whisk the eggs and cream until light and fluffy.

Add remaining ingredients, season and whisk to combine.

Pour across 4 x 5cm silicone moulds.

Cook at 160ºC, for 7 minutes.

Test the centre of one with a toothpick. When the toothpick removes clean, the eggs have set.

Nutritional Information

	Per Serve
Calories	265.1
Kilojoules	1113.3
Total Fat	21.6g
– Saturated Fat	10.3g
Sodium	493.5mg
Carbohydrates	1.5g
– Sugar	1.4g
Fibre	0.2g
Protein	17.1g

Air Fryer Boiled Egg & Crispy Bacon

Serves 1

Believe it or not both bacon & eggs can be cooked in the air fryer. Although, most of the time, I will simply boil the egg whilst cooking the bacon, eliminating the constant hovering over a hot pan and all the splattering grease. **Bacon** in the air fryer – IS SIMPLY THE BEST!

- 1 large egg (51g)
- 2 slices rindless bacon (100g)

Place the egg in the air fryer basket and cook at 150°C, 12 minutes for a soft yolk, 15 minutes for a firm yolk.

Remove with tongs and add the bacon strips.

Cook at 200°C, for 10 minutes, flipping halfway through.

OPTIONAL: If you want to cook more than one batch of bacon, make sure you drain the grease from the air fryer after each cook as it will start to smoke.

26.2g Fat
1.7g Carbs

Scrambled Eggs
Serves 1

- 2 eggs (51g each)
- 2 tbsp. (40g) cream
- 2 tbsp. (40g) cheddar cheese
- 1 tsp. (1g) chives

In a bowl crack the eggs. Add the cream and season. Whisk to combine. Add cheese and chives and pour into a lightly greased small 12cm ceramic dish. Place in air fryer basket and cook at 180°C, for 5 minutes. Lightly stir and cook for another 3 minutes. Use a fork to fluff when serving.

Nutritional Information

	Per Serve
Calories	302.9
Kilojoules	1272.3
Total Fat	22.8g
– Saturated Fat	8.2g
Sodium	1424.5mg
Carbohydrates	0.5g
– Sugar	0.5g
Fibre	0g
Protein	24.6g

Breakfast

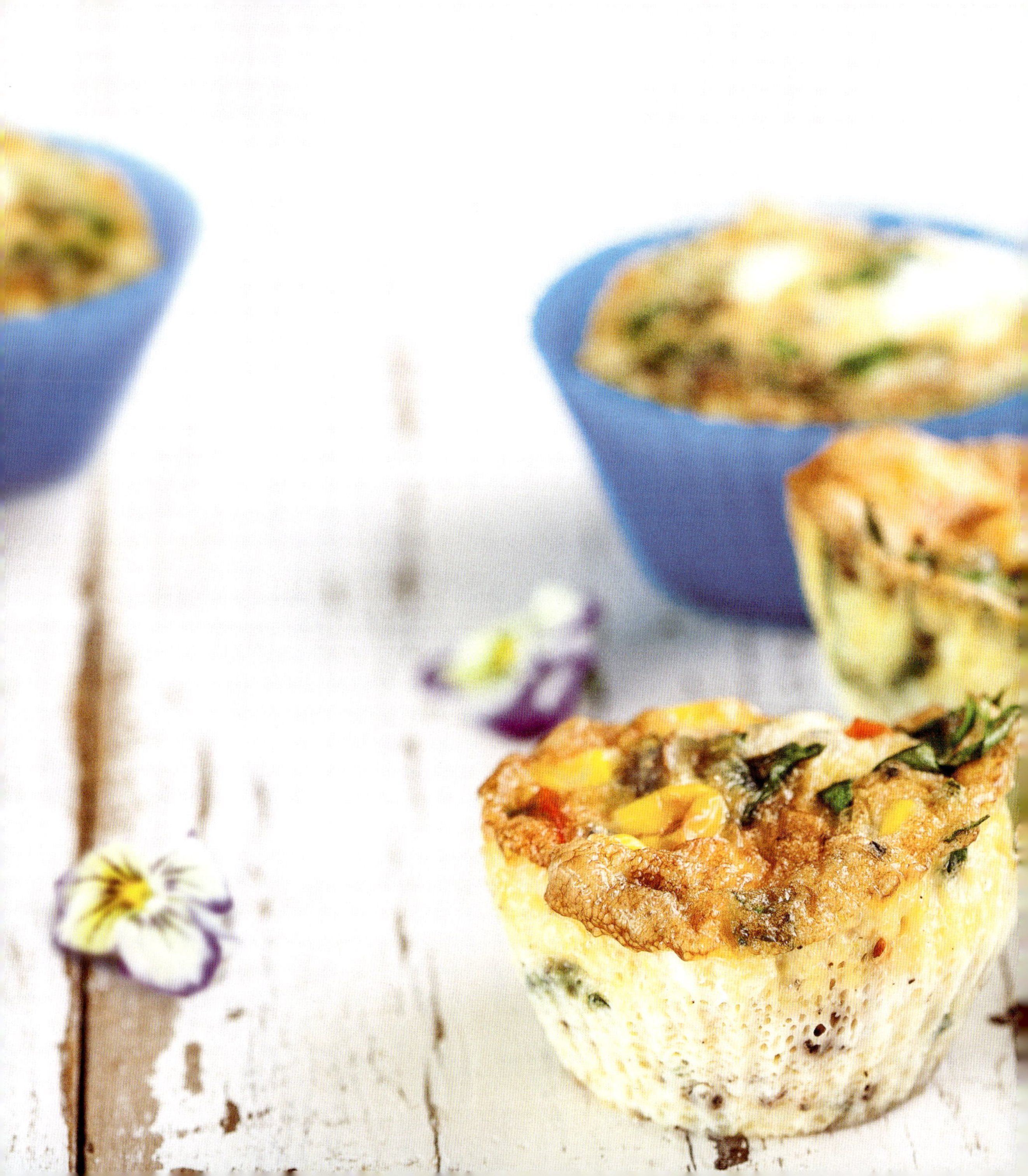

Cream Cheese & Salmon Bagels

To make these yummy bagels see p.25 and simply top with cream cheese, salmon and fresh dill. Season and serve.

12.2g Fat
1.9g Carbs

Haloumi & Toms

I recently posted this on the 4 Ingredients Facebook page, IT WAS SO POPULAR!

Cut a block of haloumi into triangles. Top each with a cherry tomato and season with pepper. Cook at 180ºC, for 8 minutes. Flip, cook for 4 minutes. Serve with fresh parsley or thyme.

Blackened Salmon

27.2g Fat
2.8g Carbs

Take 2 salmon fillets. Brush with melted butter. Sprinkle generously with Cajun seasoning. Cook at 180ºC, for 8 minutes.

THANK GOD IT'S *Fry-day!*

Healthy Keto Air Frying

Tips 4 Air Frying

1. Preheat the air fryer – 180ºC for 3 minutes – helps cook food quicker.
2. Leave space between the food so the air can reach all sides.
3. If you are cooking for a lot of people, cook in batches. Place the cooked food on a side plate and cover with foil.
4. If using baking paper, cut it to size. The heating element is in the top of the machine, so be sure to keep paper clear of it.

Air Fryer Steak
tender & juicy

Air Fryer Pork Chops
done in 12 minutes

Air Fryer Fish or Salmon
a family favourite

Air Fryer Chicken Tenders
perfect for dipping

Air Fryer Chicken Wings
ready in 30 minutes

Air Fryer Roast Chicken
crisp & juicy

Vegetables

	Temp.	Time
Asparagus	200ºC	5
Beetroot	200ºC	40
Broccoli	200ºC	6
Brussels Sprouts	190ºC	15
Carrots	190ºC	15
Cauliflower	200ºC	12
Corn on the Cob	195ºC	6
Eggplant	200ºC	15
Green Beans	200ºC	5
Kale Leaves	125ºC	12
Mushrooms	200ºC	5 – 7
Onions	200ºC	10
Peppers	200ºC	15
Potatoes	200ºC	15
Squash	200ºC	12
Sweet Potato	190ºC	30 – 35
Tomatoes	175ºC	4 – 6
Zucchini	200ºC	12

Frozen Foods

	Temp.	Time
Chicken Nuggets	200ºC	10
Crumbed Prawns	200ºC	9
Fish Fillet	200ºC	14
Fish Fingers	200ºC	10
French Fries	200ºC	14 – 18
Mozzarella Sticks	200ºC	8
Onion Rings	200ºC	8

Cooking Times & Temperatures

Meat & Seafood

	Temp.	Time
Bacon	200ºC	5 – 10
Burgers	185ºC	16 – 20
Calamari	190ºC	5 – 7
Chicken Breast	195ºC	12 –15
Chicken Drumsticks / Thighs	190ºC	30 – 40
Chicken Tenders	180ºC	8 – 10
Chicken Wings	200ºC	20 – 30
Eye Fillet Roast	195ºC	45 – 55
Filet Mignon	200ºC	18
Fish Fillet	200ºC	10
Flank Steak	200ºC	12
Meatballs	200ºC	5 – 8
Pork Chops	200ºC	12
Pork Loin	180ºC	55
Prawns	200ºC	5
Rib Eye	200ºC	10 – 15
Salmon Fillet	190ºC	12
Sausages	190ºC	15
Scallops	200ºC	5 – 7
Tenderloin	185ºC	15
Tuna Steak	200ºC	7 – 10
Whole Chicken	180ºC	60 – 70

To oil or not to oil? You do in fact need to use a little oil when cooking certain foods in the air fryer. As a general rule, you need about 1 – 2 teaspoons for most items, or 1 – 2 tablespoons for breaded/crumbed items that you want to get really crispy.

Spraying with a light mist of oil either at the start or halfway through cooking gets the best crisp on most foods. Obviously fatty meats, cakes, muffins, etc. don't require misting, but frozen foods, coated foods or fresh vegetables will for a golden finish.

Preheat your air fryer when baking cakes, muffins and using pastry. Many recipes call for preheating the air fryer, but as a general rule I tend to only preheat when I'm baking, and will often cover with alfoil for most of the cooking time to prevent burning its lid. Also bring eggs and butter to room temperature first.

Monitor the cooking process the first time you use your air fryer – it's just good practice. Some air fryers cook at higher temperatures than they report, while other air fryers may have their racks positioned closer to their heating elements. Every air fryer is different, so keep a close eye on the food you are making first time and adjust timings and temperatures as needed.

Don't overcrowd the basket – you want your food to turn out crispy. To achieve this, hot air needs to circulate around the food. To ensure this, cook your food in batches or shake, toss and turn through the cooking process or invest in a bigger air fryer.

Reheating leftovers is best done in your air fryer than anywhere else. Your pizza stays crispy on the bottom while melting the cheese on top, vegetables and fries are re-crisped to perfection, bread rolls refreshed in minutes. To be honest, most solid food is better reheated in the air fryer than anywhere else.

Be careful with light foods as each air fryer has a powerful fan built into the top of the unit. This might cause some lighter weighed foods to be swept up in the circulating air. Some foods may need to be grounded by a trivet.

There is no bottom element – that is why many recipes ask you to shake, toss or turn during the cooking process. Take for example, a pie. Sure you can cook a pie in the air fryer, but because there is no bottom heating element, you may not get a brown crispy base unless you turn it during the cooking process.

Practice makes perfect – as with all new appliances just start to use your air fryer. Don't be discouraged by 1 or 2 disasters, as you get to know your machine and how fast it cooks, you will start to experiment. This was my journey, now my air fryer sits on my kitchen counter top all the time.

The Rise & Rise *Continued* of the Air Fryer

These two pages are straight out of my book The Easiest Air Fryer Book Ever! I have included them here too, because the information is really helpful. If you want to air fry successfully, take 5 minutes and read the following first – guaranteed – it will help.

HOW DOES AN AIR FRYER WORK?

Air fryers' unique 'Rapid Air Technology' allows you to prepare food using only AIR.

Combining fast, precise, circulating hot air, the right temperatures and a grill element, air fryers allow you to fry, roast, bake and grill all kinds of delicious food.

It is this fast moving, hot air inside the air fryer basket that does the cooking; leaving food golden and crispy on the outside and lovely and moist on the inside.

BENEFITS OF AN AIR FRYER

Because you are only using air to fry

- It is much safer, no hot spitting oil
- It eliminates the smell of fried oil throughout your home
- It is economical as less ingredients and less time are required to cook successfully
- But possibly the biggest of all benefits – it is a healthier way of cooking as they help remove high-fat and high-calorie oils from the 'frying' process. Maintaining a healthy diet isn't easy when you love snack foods like hot chips, hot dogs and chicken wings, which are generally high in saturated fats (fats that are solid at room temp). It's not a miracle appliance that suddenly makes all those fatty foods good for you, but an air fryer will help you eat healthier versions of your favourite guilty-pleasures because they use a fraction of the oil compared to deep fryers without compromising flavours and textures.

TIPS TO USING AN AIR FRYER SUCCESSFULLY

Consult your manual before you start cooking. There are many different air fryer brands and models on the market and each is different. Your manual is crucial to helping you understand your particular air fryer, it is a wealth of information and often provides general cook times for certain foods. Use this information when deciding the perfect cook times and temperatures when starting out.

Contents

Introduction	03
Guide to Weights & Measures	**04**
The Rise & Continued Rise of the Air Fryer	06
Cooking Times & Temperatures	**08**
Healthy Keto Air Frying	10
Breakfast	**12**
Snacks	28
Lunch	**50**
Sides	76
Dinner	**90**
Dessert	126
Bibliography	**141**
Index	142

Guide to Weights & Measures

To help a recipe turn out right, you need to measure right.
I have included this simple conversion table to help, regardless of where you are in the world.

Grams - pounds & ounces

Grams (g)	Ounces (oz.)	Grams (g)	Ounces (oz.)
5 g	¼ oz.	225 g	9 oz.
10 g	½ oz.	250 g	10 oz.
25 g	1 oz.	275 g	11 oz.
50 g	2 oz.	300 g	12 oz.
75 g	3 oz.	325 g	13 oz.
100 g	4 oz.	350 g	14 oz.
125 g	5 oz.	375 g	15 oz.
150 g	6 oz.	400 g	1 pound (lb.)
175 g	7 oz.	700 g	1½ lb.
200 g	8 oz.	900 g	2 lb.

Spoons - millilitres (ml)

1 teaspoon	5 ml
1 dessertspoon	10 ml
1 tablespoon	15 ml

Cups - ml - fluid ounces - tablespoons

Cups	ml	Fluid Ounces	Tbsp.
⅛ cup	30 ml	1 fl oz.	2
¼ cup	60 ml	2 fl oz.	4
⅓ cup	80 ml	2.5 fl oz.	5.5
½ cup	125 ml	4 fl oz.	8
⅔ cup	160 ml	5 fl oz.	10.5
¾ cup	190 ml	6 fl oz.	12
1 cup	250 ml	8 fl oz.	16

KETO in an AIR FRYER

By now, many of you will have either a copy of **4 Ingredients Keto** – or – **The Easiest Air Fryer Book Ever!** Both bestsellers in their own rights.

People keep asking me 'Are they crazes?' There's the **ketogenic diet craze** – and – there's the **air fryer craze,** and from my perspective these **'crazes'** aren't about to disappear. In fact, they're gaining in popularity and if you merge the two, you enter into the whole new versatile and delectable world of **The Easiest Air Fryer Keto Book Ever!**

Air fryers circulate hot air to cook food. Essentially you place food in an air fryer basket, and when you turn it on, hot air rushes down and around the food. This rapid circulation of hot air makes the food you are cooking crisp – much like deep-frying, but without the oil.

The Ketogenic Diet, also known as **'Keto'** is a super-popular and restrictive diet plan that calls for lots of fat, some protein, and very few carbohydrates. The goal of this macronutrient imbalance is to keep your body in a fat-burning mode known as **ketosis.**

Everyone is distinct and a nutritious healthy diet for one will look completely different for another. But if you love the food you can eat on a Keto diet, and the ease and rapidity of air frying, then the chances are you will love the recipes within **The Easiest Air Fryer Keto Book Ever!**

Happy Air Frying – Keto style!

Kim